The Writer's Experience

The Writer's Experience

Essays on Self and Circumstance
in the Hispanic Literatures

Peter G. Earle

Lewisburg
Bucknell University Press

#628975 70

Associated University Presses
2010 Eastpark Boulevard
Cranbury, NJ 08512

The paper used in this publication meets the requirements of the American National Standard for Permanence of Paper for Printed Library Materials. Z39.48-1984.

Library of Congress Cataloging-in-Publication Data

Earle, Peter G.
    The writer's experience : essays on self and circumstance in the Hispanic literatures / Peter G. Earle.
        p.   cm.
    Includes bibliographical references and index.
    ISBN-10: 0-8387-5660-3 (alk. paper)
    ISBN-13: 978-0-8387-5660-7 (alk. paper)
    1. Spanish American literature—History and criticism.   2. Spanish literature—History and criticism.   3. Self in literature.   I. Title.
    PQ7081.E273   2006
    860.9'353—dc22   2006000767

PRINTED IN THE UNITED STATES OF AMERICA

Para Beba, ". . . dulce compañía"

Form ever follows function, and this is the law.
—Louis Henry Sullivan, Architect

Contents

Foreword

A<small>T A MEETING WITH STUDENTS OF THE UNIVERSITY OF PENNSYLVANIA IN</small> 2004, Norman Mailer remarked that a writer's knowledge—of the kind he or she really needs—comes from "the life you can't escape."

Mailer's statement can be taken as a stimulus to serious readers and critics, as well as to other creative writers. With all its stumbling blocks and confusions, "the life you can't escape" invites the author's double exercise of *memory* and *imagination*. It incites or inspires as much as it frustrates or restricts. It shows in infinite ways how circumstances affect both the creative process and its perception by readers.

Since the middle of the twentieth century a lot of research on literature in the Hispanic world has minimized or lost sight of "the life you can't escape" as the critic's and literary historian's primary interest. Indifference to biographical sources became increasingly apparent after about 1960 in scholarly studies, manuals and journals concerned with literature in Spain and Hispanic America.

My point of departure in these essays is the writer's experience—personal, social, cultural, political, and historical—rather than the postmodern and post-structuralist theories as practiced by scholars of the late twentieth century. A paradox emerges from modern applications of semiotics, foreseen as the *doctrine of signs* by John Locke in the eighteenth century and elaborated much later by Ferdinand de Saussure, and then the Prague, Russian, and French structuralist schools—as "*a science* [i.e., semiology] *that studies the life of signs with society.*"

The paradox of signs that emerge from creative writing is this: Spirited discussions have concentrated on the nature and status of language as a new category of science, including the extent to which a literary text can be seen as self-reflecting or autonomous. But the vital connections between what is experienced and perceived in an author's life, and what is subsequently (and consequently) ex-

9

pressed in a poem, narrative, text, or essay have too often been obscured or forgotten amid the post-structuralist scholars' fascination with signs that ignores all they consider to be a writer's intended *meanings* and that writer's personal *circumstances*. The process of sign-analysis leads mostly to other signs, and usually an intellectual dead end.

An author's explicit and implicit *autobiography* (to the degree that an inquiring reader can identify it) is the legitimate basis and primary motivation of what is written. As it applies to investigation and criticism, it should be emphasized, "autobiography" has a generating function that, in turn, invites the reader's engagement in the author's function as historian, witness of other lives, spiritual observer and cultural commentator.

Some twenty years ago in a graduate course on the Hispanic-American novel I recommended reading Gabriel García Márquez's conversations with Plinio Apuleyo Mendoza—published in *El olor de la guayaba* (1982)—for a better understanding of the Colombian novelist's creative process. Immediately a devotee of post-structuralist method raised her hand and asked, "What's the point of it, if authors are the least qualified to explain what functions in their works?" I answered that even if from the 1960s to the 1980s García Márquez wasn't interested in literary theory and its most hallucinating fashions (and he really wasn't and isn't), he's still the primary source for knowledge of the conditions, enthusiasms and disillusions that affect the composition of his works.

The creator of *Cien años de soledad* is not alone in this. Like Cervantes, Emily Dickinson, Tolstoy, Mark Twain, Thomas Mann, Virginia Woolf, Gabriela Mistral, Hemingway, García Lorca, Neruda, Carlos Fuentes, Elena Garro, Alejo Carpentier, Isabel Allende, and Ernesto Cardenal, he consistently *reveals* (to anyone seriously interested) the situations and obsessions that have incited him to write.

I believe that our primary function as conscientious readers, critics, and intellectual biographers is closer to the *detective's* than to the theorist's. We're poorly served by ideas and systems that bypass or intentionally exclude the writing artist's relationships, motives, expectations, and (Julio Cortázar be praised) the antics and suggestions of his or her *cronopios*. Our ethical and aesthetic responsibility as persistent detectives is to verify and illuminate the conversion of those incitements into works of art. Novels, stories and poems are long or short transformations of autobiographies—or, seen in another light, absorbent testimonies.

Following Ortega y Gasset (whose intellectual presence is evident in this book) in his illuminating egocentricity, we can say that each author is the writing artist and his or her circumstance, *and*—also— the aggregate of his or her memories. As Elena Garro's narrator expresses it at the beginning of *Los recuerdos del porvenir* (1963): "I'm no more than my memory and the memory that others have of me." In his "Essay on Aesthetics as a Prologue" appearing in *La deshumanización del arte y otros ensayos estéticos,* Ortega reminds us that all that can be observed belongs to *someone*: "*I* means, then, not this man as distinguished from another, still less a man distinguished from things, but everything—men, things, situations—in the process of verification, being, realization."[1] For emphasis he adds: "Everything, viewed from within, is *I.*"

The reader/detective (in the freest, autonomous sense of the term) believes that everything of importance can be explained on the basis of conditions and forces that affect the writer. Cervantes condensed his aggregation of experiences in *Don Quijote* and the *Novelas ejemplares.* Benito Pérez Galdós did the same from the 1870s to the 1890s in his *Episodios nacionales* and *Novelas contemporáneas.*

For his part José Vasconcelos energetically relives—in *Ulises criollo* (1935) and its three sequels—his political and amorous adventures of the Mexican Revolution and the postrevolutionary era.

And even a casual reading of the first volume of García Márquez's autobiography, *Vivir para contarla* (2002), shows us the close relationship between his youthful acquaintances and experiences and the inventions and ironies in his novels and stories. As a young journalist in Colombia the author of *Cien años de soledad* met circus performers, ill-starred politicians, soccer players, wayward priests and softhearted courtesans (one of whom had "a secret door and humanitarian rates for repentant clerics").

In *Canto general* (1950)—Pablo Neruda demonstrates a historical memory as prodigious as that of Tolstoy, Dos Passos, or the Colombian novelist just mentioned. In the concluding poem—"Termino aquí (1949)"—he describes his panorama articulated in over six hundred pages as a form of self-liberation: "Por fin, soy libre adentro de los seres." In its fifteen cantos he has invoked with humanitarian emphasis the evolution of Hispanic America from its geological origins to its contemporary conflagrations.

Every writer exercises, in varied proportion, two functions: one can be called assertive, or *dominant*; the other receptive, or *assimilative*. A balance is needed—precarious as it often is—between the author's imperative ego and the intrusive creatures and caprices that infiltrate his or her work. I recall that in Latin and old Spanish *autor* and *actor* were often confused or used interchangeably, and that in my 1970 edition of the Royal Academy's *Diccionario de la lengua española* the suggestive archaism *auctor* still appears. The persistent little *c*, in effect, combines the writer's two main components (author and actor) in one creative function.

Thus, some (dominant) writers impose themselves simultaneously as authors and actors. Think of Vasconcelos, self-appointed "Mexican Ulysses," temperamental romantic and political actvist; of Miguel de Unamuno, exhibitor of his philosophical doubts and spiritual anxieties in *Del sentimiento trágico* (1913) and *San Manuel Bueno, mártir* (1933); of Julio Cortázar, director or puppeteer of the endearing creatures he calls *cronopios* and his more autonomous eccentrics in *Rayuela* (1963) the untiring animus of his alter-ego, Horacio Oliveira. Think also of Walt Whitman, Gabriela Mistral and Pablo Neruda and their respective songs of themselves; and of José Martí, who aspired to promote—in spirit, ideas and action—a new, truly independent Hispanic America.

Other (assimilative) writers prefer remaining on the periphery: Cervantes mainly lets Don Quijote and Sancho and a varied selection of other characters do the talking, fantasizing, and cutting up; in the three books of John Dos Passos's *U.S.A.* (1938) a whole nation expresses itself as a hesitant and widely varied chorus; in *La muerte de Artemio Cruz* (1962) Carlos Fuentes gives his protagonist free reign to remember, rave, magnify, and trivialize, as well as to corrupt himself and others. And, incorporating the personal dynamism of two famous figures—Carlota, Empress of Mexico and the Americas; and Eva Perón, Savior of the Dispossessed, Patroness of the Pampa, etc.—Fernando del Paso wrote *Noticias del Imperio* (1987) and Tomás Eloy Martínez gave us *Santa Evita* (1994). In the two latter works the authors show how fact, legend, and myth merge and enliven the Mexican and Argentine collective memories.

In the chapters that follow I attempt to find a closer relationship between the authors' biographical and historical circumstances—on the one hand—and their representative published works—on the other—than most academic critics in recent decades have thought necessary.

The need is clear. For example, consider the uses of magic. Borges, Elena Garro, and García Márquez all practice it in their narratives. But each one develops it in a unique way (i.e., affected by different perceptions and personal concerns) and as required in the stories of *Ficciones* and *El aleph*, the episodes of *Los recuerdos del porvenir*, and those of *Cien años de soledad*. Also, Neruda's *Canto general*, Martí's *Cartas de Nueva York*, Isabel Allende's *La casa de los espíritus*, and Vasconcelos' *Ulises criollo* were all written in exile; but, like the instruments of magic, the uses of memory and autobiography differ widely in each work.

Convinced as I am of the importance of personal experience and historical memory in literature (What would Vasconcelos have given us without his relationship to the Mexican Revolution? Or Elena Garro without the influence of her chaotically eccentric family?[2] Or Tomás Eloy Martínez without the preceding political cavalcade of Eva and Juan Domingo Perón), I have also been motivated for this book by recent Hispanic writers' seldom-recognized role (both in Spain and Hispanic America) as *initiators*. It should be recalled that well before Alice Hoffman wrote her magical *The Probable Future* (2005) in which beds of swamp flowers wilt when observed by human eyes and thirteen generations of girls acquire with puberty, unique vision, and freedom from pain, García Márquez and Isabel Allende had already given us the generational quirks and tricks of their own best-known narrative creations. Also, we shouldn't forget that in his theory and practice of the autonomous short-story character, Horacio Quiroga preceded Ernest Hemingway's "The Killers," and Eudora Welty's "The Worn Path." (See chapter 6, "Circling the Aleph . . ."); and that the Hispanic-American vanguards in poetry, as practiced by Vicente Huidobro and César Vallejo developed simultaneously with (not after) French surrealism. Spain and Hispanic America, as seedbeds of magical visions and a fascination with the extravagant (Ramón del Valle Inclán's *esperpento*, modern-day alchemy, Borges's elusive Aleph, the truculence of home-grown politics in many short stories and novels) have consistently called for direct interpretation, based on direct, intense experience.

Whether the writer's direct experience and imposed environment will ultimately be recognized as the necessary basis of whatever theory ensues remains to be seen. That's a question for writers and readers of new times, trends, and cultures to answer.

Meanwhile, Ortega y Gasset's growing identity problem in the Hispanic world (chapter 5), the spiritual intensity of Vasconcelos' Martí's and Mistral's political devotions (chapter 10), Borges's ironic view of the poetic process in the most ingenious of his stories (chapter 6), and Michel Foucault's plea to diminish the figure and function of Don Quijote to the arid status of "nothing but language" (chapter 1) are samples of the realities and circumstances that as serious readers (in this life we can't escape) we should be dealing with.

Acknowledgments

SHORTER VERSIONS OF SIX OF THESE ESSAYS WERE FIRST PUBLISHED UNDER the following titles:

"Octavio Paz: poesía e historia," *Nueva Revista de Filología Hispánica*, 40, no. 2 (1992), was rewritten as Chapter Three: "Octavio Paz and the Circumstances of Poetry."

"Ortega y Gasset in Argentina: The Exasperating Colony," *Hispania*, 70, no. 3 (1987), as chapter 5 [same title].

"Perspectivas creadoras, el cuento," *Ideas/Imágenes*, cultural supplement of *La Nueva Provincia*, Bahía Blanca, Argentina (March 18, 1999), as chapter 6: "Circling the Aleph: Hispanic American Short Stories."

"On the Contemporary Displacement of the Hispanic American Essay," *Hispanic Review*, 46, no. 3 (1978), as chapter 7: "As the Fly Spies: Hispanic American Essays."

"Resonancias del 98," *Ideas/Imágenes*, cultural supplement of *La Nueva Provincia*, Bahía Blanca, Argentina (February 5, 1998), as chapter 8: "Spain's Edgy Generation."

"In and Out of Time (Cervantes, Dostoyevsky, Borges)," *Hispanic Review*, 71, no. 1 (2003), as chapter 9: "In and Out of Time (Cervantes, Dostoyevsky, Borges, García Márquez)."

The Writer's Experience

1
Figure and Function
in Hispanic-American Literature

> Un hombre se propone la tarea de dibujar el mundo . . .
>
> —Jorge Luis Borges

FIGURE AND FUNCTION ARE THE PRINCIPAL FORCES IN LITERATURE. THE two words invite many definitions, analogies and synonyms. Figure, for example, can be a venerable or notorious person; an emblem, symbol or metaphor; a graphic representation, idiom or gesture; a religious icon, historic building, celestial body or scene of ruin. It's the image that remains with us after a particular encounter, experience or reading.

Function, in turn, is really figuration. It's an action that gives life to the text. We find it in prehistoric drawings of the hunt, interstate traffic patterns, and bird flights. Figuration derives in Latin from *figmentum* ("image") and *figura* ("shape") and figure—it turns out—is related to fiction, which comes from *fingere* ("to fashion"). Those signs emerging from philological curiosity amount to a paradox. That is, the magic of literature is found in the nonverbal phenomena that underlie and surpass it.

Literary roots and incitements are to be found elsewhere, outside language. Many decades before our academic fascination with self-reflecting texts, José Martí (1853–95) showed his awareness that the power of a text is its ability to reflect everything outside itself. In a letter to his daughter María in New York in April 1895 (a little over a month before he would die in battle in eastern Cuba), he wrote: "Where I find true poetry is in scientific books, in the life of the world, in the world's order, in the ocean's depths, in the tree's music, integrity and strength, in love, in the sky's dimensions and its family of stars,—and in the unity of a universe that encloses so many

19

different things. Yet all things are one, and reflect in the evening's light the day's productive work."[1] Martí was an exemplar of figurative writing. In his elegy for Ralph Waldo Emerson (1882) the Cuban poet and essayist pointed out that nature produces requirements as well as marvels and that art is no more and no less than "nature created by man." Like Whitman and Neruda, Martí had panoramic vision, and within his poetically controlled abundance he consistently practiced a kind of creative benevolence. Beauty for him was a harmony of figure and function in which nineteenth-century creators and their imagery—not to forget their democratic awakenings—were enhanced by hopes of a fuller cultural life. Beauty consisted of visions that were metaphors of what was necessary and good.

Ethics were inseparable from aesthetics. Had he been born fifty or a hundred years later, Martí could not have accepted Ortega y Gasset's concept of dehumanized art, nor the abstractionist leanings of most late twentieth-century literary theory. He had heard and seen the appropriate sounds, figures and colors that resulted in his particular language: his extended signature elaborated in rhythm and vision—so to speak—and in the intensity of his self-portrait.

These thoughts on the priority of the figure as subject, actor, author, observer, thinker, master, profile, victim, or object in Hispanic-American literature have occupied me for a long time. Consider them the compulsions of a reader who believes that literary theory has often neglected the figure's vital functions. Theory is counterproductive when it numbs the senses or distracts the reader from what he or she is reading. Some ethic and aesthetic considerations lost in the frenzies of postmodern analysis remain valid. For example, personal judgment is still a virtue that can surpass simplistic impressionism. But it needs to be based on a level of intellectual experience that discerns social and cultural patterns and makes a reasonable distinction between creative achievement and creative failure. Personal judgment (i.e., an adequate blend of the subjective and the objective as one faces the circumstances at hand) is still the vital center of literary criticism. Literary theory, no matter how meticulously we formulate it, is inherently tentative and always vulnerable to the pitfalls of the abstract.

Our precarious status as teachers, critics and editors in an allegedly postmodern era could be compared to that of the New Yorker's memorable humorist James Thurber, who in his introduction to *My*

Life and Hard Times mentions his propensity since early youth to stumble and fall down. He candidly attributes that phenomenon to his "habit" of walking into himself. Real or imagined, Thurber's dilemma could serve as a metaphor for what has happened to a lot of academic criticism. Why have so many university scholars lost their way in a wilderness of philosophical indeterminacy? Why have the poet, storyteller and essayist and the product of their efforts so often been slighted in the name of textual deconstruction and the vacillating search for an unidentifiable phantom called "the Other"? What purpose is served in following Jonathan Culler's and Roland Barthes' mysterious dictum that literature should "unexpress [*sic*] the expressible"? It was always my candid impression that literature's basic function was just the opposite, to express (i.e., to shout, whisper, insinuate, point out, elaborate, imply, or reconstruct) a reaction to everything it encountered—whether "expressible" or not. In their theoretic zeal, Culler and Barthes and most postmodernists have succumbed to the temptation of walking into themselves. But in the process they've obviously lacked Thurber's and Charlie Chaplin's gift of comic self-awareness, and the literary work at hand is usually slighted, if not bypassed altogether.

As a refugee from the heartland of postmodern discourse and a disbeliever in the self-reflecting text I'm inevitably attracted by the figure that prevails—or hides, frolics, or agonizes—not just in the rigid confines of the Text, but in all the microintimacies and outward reaches of the Work.

Consider the two terms. Text is an extract or abstract: the explicated or exploited medium and instrument, the graphic thing before our eyes composed of written or printed characters and punctuation marks. It's that and nothing more. Work (opus, opera, *obra*) has active, operative, protean connotations. It's an entirety: it embraces the world that reverberates within, around and at varying distances from a text; it synthesizes the process of invention and representation that a writer articulates for a reader.

The figure is what matters most in any work. It beckons, first to its author, then its reader. Think of her, him or it as the dynamics of what Aristotle and Plato called *persona*, a necessarily flexible yet substantial presence of the author and his or her company of images, masks, creatures and gestures. *Persona*, in that sense, is the nucleus of a poem or narrative.

Ideas, themes, and structures do not generate figures. The opposite is true. In *Don Quijote* (part 2, chapter 17) the errant knight and paladin of universal justice confronts and challenges a bedraggled lion in an open cage. In response, Cervantes allows the somnolent animal to turn and lie down with its buttocks insensitively facing the Knight of Doleful Countenance. Quijote, the paragon of noble intentions, is thereby disdained—or is he dignified?—by the lion's passivity. The encounter is really a *desencuentro*, a disengagement or comic displacement of the individual human will by a figure (one of many throughout Cervantes' novel) of the world's dogged, post-chivalric Ambiguity.[2]

The figure is the point at which history, reality, and the imagination aesthetically merge. It can refer to things and situations as well as to people and other creatures. It's equally at home in fable, allegory, or novel; in news report, poem or essay; in court trial, advertisement, or baseball game. In the movements and personalities of baseball, figure skating, and other athletic formats one can admire its inseparability from function. Many seasons ago, on a summer afternoon of the early twentieth century, a brash young center fielder, Casey Stengel, came to bat at Ebbets Field in Brooklyn, always a public inferno for visiting teams. Foreseeing the Dodger fans' unruly reception and standing straight at the plate amid a solid chorus of boos, he lifted his cap to full arm's length and let a bird fly out. With all the appearance of spontaneity, Casey had made himself the author, emblem, and actor of an artistic moment. His definitive act— the gesture of hand, cap and liberated bird—was comedy in action, finely tuned and timed: a fine athletic equivalent of literary expression. Stengel, who years later as an accomplished team manager became famous for his convoluted elocution, was already a poet and probably didn't know it. Further, he had shown in a clearly unintellectual milieu how much he had in common with diverse Hispanic-American fictional characters in symbolic movements and poses of their own.

Think of Demetrio Macías, already dead in the final scene of Mariano Azuela's novel, *Los de abajo* (1916), but still propped against a rock, gripping his rifle and aiming it at an enemy no longer present. Or old Viscacha, the rodent-like rogue and tutor of Martín Fierro's second son, recalled and admiringly described by the latter in part 2 of José Hernández's narrative poem (1870, 1879): el Viejo Viscacha, whose farewell gesture (following a makeshift shallow burial on the pampa) was a protruding hand that would later be eaten by stray dogs. Think of virtually all Gabriel García Márquez's characters in their shifting realm of historical absurdity, of Gabriela Mistral's cradle rhythms and her consistently maternal demeanor, of José Martí's impressionistic portraits of North and South American "representative men." Remember also Julia de Burgos' poetry as an augury, and her gravitation toward suicide in New York.

In every large dictionary, including *Oxford*, *Random House* and *Webster's International*, figure has more definitions than either character or person. Further, it's a verb as well as a noun and noun-in-apposition, and as a noun can be the synonym of symbol, form, emblem, or image, or a person of distinction, notoriety, or impressive mediocrity. Through movement and form, figure connotes self-generation or manipulation by some hidden force, something that draws the artist or writer into a collaborative project of renewal and modification. First with the writing, then the reading—plus the reading that precedes and accompanies all writing—metaphors and symbols spring forth, like opening buds on a tree. Metaphors, that is, the graphic representations of people or the symbolic objects associated with them, also are figures and wield great suggestive, transformational power. Consider these examples:

1. The gold chamber pots in Sir Thomas More's *Utopia* (book 2, chapter 6) and in Gabriel García Márquez's *Cien años de soledad* (the novel in which a commode with the family coat of arms encrusted on the bottom is used by Fernanda del Carpio) are made from a mineral seen by both authors as a degraded rather than precious commodity. More and García Márquez disdainfully utilize the expensive receptacles as a critique of human greed and Freudian self-aggrandizement.

2. In Julio Cortázar's ironic testimony, "Turismo aconsejable" (*Ultimo round*, vol. I) an old woman—maybe sleeping, maybe dead—with flies walking undisturbed over her face is seated at the base of a utility pole on a crowded square in Calcutta.

3. In Jorge Luis Borges' story "El aleph" the small prismatic device installed under the stairs in Carlos Argentino Daneri's basement, which (Daneri alleges and the poet-narrator "Borges" is disposed to believe) enables the observer to contemplate the universe in all its complexities, simultaneously and from every angle ("desde todos los puntos"). As most readers familiar with Borges' literary relationships are aware, the author has used the *aleph* and its owner to ridicule an academically influential but poetically ungifted Argentine author and editor of the 1930s and 1940s.

4. The central figure in the third and final part of Octavio Paz's essay *Posdata* is a truncated pyramid: an image of human cruelty and sacrifice that remains—in the aftermath of a massacre at Tlatelolco, Mexico City in October, 1968—the mirror and abode of the most terrifying Mexican god, Huitzilopochtli, and his snake-woman mother, Coatlicue. Thus the pyramid with its sacrificial top is a figure, Paz tells us, of a collective masochism, a twentieth-century fascination with the varied phenomena of self-destruction. "We adore the image that crushes us."

5. In José Martí's foreword to *Versos libres* we read "*El verso ha de ser como una espada reluciente, que deja a los espectadores la memoria de un guerrero que va camino al cielo, y al envainarla en el sol, se rompe en alas.*" ("The line of a poem should be like a gleaming sword, leaving with its observers the image of a warrior moving skyward and who, as he plunges it into the sun, bursts into wings.").

Figures are necessarily the subjects and objects of Function. In turn, function is the active partnership that joins writer and reader—not just as a couple, but together with all the gods, demons, demiurges or magical forces that may have influenced each in the transmission and reception of any genre. The British-Utopian and Colombian-socialite chamber pots, the phantasmagoric *aleph*, the sacrificial pyramid, the poor woman with flies on her face, and Martí's orchestration of imagery around an invented warrior's sword thrust clearly demonstrate how inseparable figure and function are. Like Casey Stengel's bird gesture or Juliet when she stabs herself shortly after Romeo's suicide (her words to the dagger—"This is thy sheath"—are really superfluous) these images speak to us nonverbally, with all the eloquence that circumstance, perception, timing and physical movement can convey.

And language? What's to be said of the words and word-clusters that are the material and literal texture of any work? Obviously, without words there can be no literature. But we need to distinguish between language as a medium and literature as the function that animates and transcends the medium. A multitude of academic readers over the past several decades have espoused and expounded language's absorbent, generative role. Why not, instead, place language in the same instrumental category as paint or clay, a violin or a mirror; that is, fully recognize it as a specific means for the achievement of communication or an artistic mission? No one can deny that words, in all kinds of contexts, wield enormous power. But, like the sword, machine gun, or most sophisticated laser weapon, they're not autonomous; human beings invented and developed them and human beings manipulate, control or abuse them. Within literature itself attempts are sometimes made to give an instrumental role to spontaneous letter-clusters. In the seventh canto of his book-length poem *Altazor*, Vicente Huidobro wants us to believe that in his peculiar creative situation Altazor the bird-man or man-bird, his airborne poetry-dispensing protagonist, can speak without words, that sounds can express emotion and sensation, even when they fail to convey meaning. Like serious writing, serious reading remains a solitary experience, because theoretic disturbances transformed themselves into a state of repetitious boredom in the last quarter of the twentieth century.

Probably the most notable distraction in academia was the deconstructive campaign initiated by Jacques Derrida, who in 1967 published his three most influential works. Happily for most of us, as Vernon W. Gras has observed in *The New Princeton Encyclopedia of Poetry and Poetics* (New York: MJL Books, 1993), 281, "To repeat deconstructive readings on various texts with always the same outcomes tends to become monotonous after the early subversive thrills have dwindled. This monotony, the result of an exhausted deconstructive model, probably will bring an end to the direct application of d. to l." Better yet, in the dawn of the twenty-first century, "the early subversive thrills" have not only dwindled but virtually disappeared. Michel Foucault, for his part, asks us to consider the tenacious but always tremulous figure of Don Quijote as "nothing but language." It's easy to agree with part of his proposition, the figurative aspect: Don Quijote is "himself like a sign, a long thin graphism, a letter that has escaped from the open pages of a book." Well, fine; at least it escaped. But as Peggy Lee plaintively asked in a song years ago, "Is that all there is?" Why as Don Quijote's readers and implicit companions should we accept this shallow dehumanization? Didn't the dynamic process that gave the author's stepson perennial life (Cervantes specifies in the first paragraph of his prologue, "I'm really not Don Quijote's father, but his stepfather") start long before that miraculous escape from open, already printed pages? Listen to Foucault as he shrinks the helpless knight into a blurred textual abstraction: "His whole being is nothing but language, text, printed pages, stories that have already been printed down. He is made up of interwoven words; he is writing itself wandering through the world among the resemblance of things." Michel Foucault, *The Order of Things* (London: Routledge Classics, 2003, p. 251).

Foucault's first flaw is his exclusion of virtually everything that matters in narrative creation, from Cervantes' known and unknown experiences and the secret voices he heard, to the necessarily unique combination of temporal and spatial factors that incited him to write in the first place.

Secondly, he errs in thinking that live beings—even when born in the imagination and/or received from other works—are "nothing but language." With the fervor of a five-year-old speculating on Santa Claus's or the tooth fairy's imminent visit, he believes without question in the autonomy of "writing itself." He fails or refuses to recognize the basic truth that a poem, essay, story, or play is a triple phenomenon: a complex, immeasurable convergence of forces that begins before the act of writing, is expressed during the act of writing, and continues operating (with unpredictable effect as readers and other writers join the process) after the act of writing. Thus, the intended self-sufficiency of Foucault's "long thin graphism" notwithstanding, Miguel de Unamuno was inspired to write his own *Life of Don Quijote and Sancho,* and Jorge Luis Borges found his ideal collaborator for a short story in the ephemeral workaholic figure of Pierre Menard, who literally lived and wrote Don Quijote on his own.

Thus, the magic reality of the world, including the achievements of the world's artists, writers and musicians, resides dynamically in the artist's or writer's or musician's ability to plot and manipulate language. The Foucaultian procedure with its encapsulated texts, superficial signs and "interwoven words" leads only to an intellectual dead end.

The basic functions in literature cannot be confined to language. Rather, they assimilate and reflect all the idiosyncrasies of the author's experience, and the critic's first obligation is to see them in relevant, circumstantial ways. These could be classified as 1) personality, 2) social condition, 3) spirit (including religious, philosophical and mythical thought), 4) politics, and 5) culture.

Culture, probably the most important of the five, can be defined as an awakening to historical circumstance, which, in turn, stimulates creative activity. In one of his finest essays, "Nota sobre la inteligencia americana," Alfonso Reyes says that the typical European writer is born on the top level of the Eiffel Tower, and that the typical Hispanic-American writer comes to life in an infernal region near the center of the earth. The contrast of images is obvious. The European, it seems, was endowed with the requisite gifts of tradition, extended geographical vision, and intellectual detachment. Not so for the Hispanic American, who begins psychologically where the Aztec martyr Cuauhtémoc ended, with his feet ceremoniously roasted for the greater glory of the Spanish Conquest and Christianity; that is in a historical subregion with no escape routes.

Remember that Alfonso Reyes was a recognized leader of the Hispanic-American intelligentsia, never their detractor. His Eiffel Tower/Inferno juxtaposition complements and is in harmony with many other literary intuitions of the Americas' historical handicaps, as seen in the works of José Martí, Ezequiel Martínez Estrada, Pablo Neruda, Octavio Paz, Gabriel García Márquez Rosario Ferré, and Isabel Allende.

Everyone in or outside the Western Hemisphere who has read or written about Hispanic America has been affected by this imposition of inferiority. G. W. F. Hegel promoted it in his *Philosophy of History*: the New World in its predetermined "immaturity" and general impotence had an awe-inspiring geography but was virtually devoid of history. The eighteenth-century naturalists Corneille De Pauw and Jean Louis Buffon preceded him in his negative view; others, including Count Keyserling and José Ortega y Gasset (see chapter 4 of this book), were to follow. Echoing all those predecessors, the Venezuelan journalist Carlos Rangel wrote in 1975 that "from Bolívar to Carlos Fuentes every thoughtful and sincere Latin American has recognized, at least at certain times, the calamity of Latin America" (*Del buen salvaje al buen revolucionario*, 7th ed. [Caracas: Monte Avila Editores, 1976, p. 22], and the Argentinean H. A. Murena in *El pecado original de América* (1954) finds a collective feeling that Latin America is actually "a form of punishment for an offense that we're unaware of." (H. A. Murena, *El pecado original de América* [Buenos Aires: Editorial Sur, 1954], p. 164). For Murena Hispanic Americans are "the dispossessed": culturally, economically and—most of all—historically. The three most recent Hispanic-American Nobel laureates complement and intensify those views of deprivation. The Colombian Gabriel García Márquez, in the mythical plagues and swamplands of his most famous novel, and the Chilean poet Pablo Neruda, in the revivalist spirit of his expansive *Canto General*, portray human existence in the New World as a perpetual struggle against

oblivion. For his part, the Mexican poet Octavio Paz sees the struggle
in terms of historical solitude and a need for cultural definition: in
El laberinto de la soledad and many subsequent essays and poems.

If restoration of the Figure to recognition in literary criticism is a
valid enterprise, the elements of characterization need to be recognized (Foucault's quick shrinkage of Don Quijote is our wake-up
call). Those elements apply to the figure in the fullest, most flexible
sense. The figure's dynamism is most forcefully present in protagonists like José Hernández's Martín Fierro, Fernando del Paso's Carlota, José Rubén Romero's Pito Pérez, Tomás Eloy Martínez's Eva
Peron, García Márquez's wheezing old Patriarch, and Elena Poniatowska's feisty Jesusa Palancares. Not to be forgotten are the writers
who consistently reveal themselves as the true protagonists of their
works: Martí, Domingo Faustino Sarmiento, Ruben Darío, Ortega y
Gasset (during his three sojourns in Buenos Aires), Gabriela Mistral,
Victoria Ocampo, César Vallejo, Eduardo Mallea, Borges, Juan
Rulfo, and Gonzalo Rojas are noticeably self-projecting authors.
They all stand out as figures in their restless curiosity and either lyric
or intellectual intensity. Like nature, literature obeys necessity; it
can't escape circumstance.

Every writer tells us, or implies, that she or he writes what *has* to
be said. Accordingly, one discerns parallels in social and cultural
trends—including fashion in music, food, clothing, and architecture—and the sense or lack of sense that we find in the concepts of
community on one hand, and of literary theory and criticism on the
other. Consider a contemporary architectural trend as a metaphor.
In a provocative book, *Home from Nowhere* (New York: Simon & Schuster, 1996), James Howard Kunstler attacks the disconnected architectural sprawl in contemporary North American life and the
benumbed mind-set that has encouraged destruction of the traditional town and replaced it with "a formless, soulless, centerless, de-
moralizing mess" (112). He finds civic and artistic hope only in "a
culture of walkable neighborhoods," in "room-like spaces out-
doors" (137).

That architectural disconnectedness configuring a mess forms
part of the postmodern system. It is anchored—snagged rather—in
indeterminacy. It's the common junkyard of deconstructive reading
and deconstructive living. Such reading wants to remove from all
"texts" (*works* go unrecognized) meanings that, it is claimed, have
already been dissolved in the process of writing: "*archi-écriture*" in

Jacques Derrida's witty but hollow pun. As Kunstler points out, such living is experienced in "single use zones" without a center, in which houses and housing units, shopping malls and supermarkets, office parks, school complexes, and fast-food restaurants face one another in jumbled symmetry. It's the architectural aspect of post-modern life in which in-communication, confusion and meaning-lessness are erected as aesthetic goals. I have thought of it as an appropriate analogy to the many academic mis-readings of Hispanic-American works. But also—more happily—a natural resistance has evolved, consisting of the vibrant immunity of an overwhelming majority of Hispanic-American writers to what scholars have been saying about their work. Indeterminacy in literature, literary criticism, video games, electronic music, and social patterns is also the void that nature is supposed to abhor, but to which a variety of writers, artists, critics, and public personages have felt a fatal attraction.

Love of the void extends even to news reporting. In January 1997, Daniel Schorr observed on National Public Radio that the trend in television news has moved more and more toward focusing on the methods and techniques—as well as on the televised figure—of the "anchor" man or woman him/her self. Thus, what is ostensibly being reported and analyzed—the facts and "issues" and the possible consequences thereof—tends to be relegated to the background. Just as in literary theory, architecture and community organization, postmodern practice in news reporting, with its emphasis on the recurring presence of the reporting figure and the increasing importance of his or her demeanor, has consistently resulted in a sacrifice of the consequential *what* to the more spectacular *how.*

Notwithstanding all that, the creative will persists, as it always will, like perennial weeds that emerge through cracks in the pavement. In 1988 I had the unprofessional but deep satisfaction of hearing Isabel Allende remark at a literary conference at Rice University that in writing *La casa de los espíritus* and everything she had published by then, she was oblivious to critical theory, past and present. Her true guides, her real collaborators, were her characters and their predicaments, the literary offspring of people she had known, the recurring figures of her extended family: Clara ("la clarividente"), who could see and foresee everything of importance; the hot-tempered reactionary landowner, Esteban Trueba; Blanca and Clara (Esteban's socially committed daughter and granddaughter), among others.

In the last analysis, "language" is little more than a system of re-flectors or sounding boards it is the instrument, the material at hand, and the writer's habitat. Authors obsessed with an idea or image, authors and their phantom company of figures, are the ones who decide what a story, poem or essay will consist of. The outline of a figure is confirmed not only by its graphic existence on pages, but by an infinity of other factors: Secret insights and epiphanies, the wellsprings of autobiography, good and bad publicity, the leg-ends of authorship, good and bad criticism, and—last but hardly least—the reader's imagination. Like distant stars that have ceased to exist, the figure's light projects itself long after it was assimilated by words and written down.

Accordingly, people and symbolic *objects* and *places* (Sarmiento's and Martínez Estrada's pampa, Carlos Fuentes' Mexico City, García Márquez's mythical marshlands, and Fernanda del Carpio's cham-ber pot, Neruda's Machu Picchu, Borges's *aleph*, Alejo Carpentier's guillotine erected in the prow of a ship arriving in the Antilles in *El siglo de las luces*) always reflect something that lies behind, within or beyond them.

And of course, the *people*, the inadvertent self-portraits as well as the invented figures, are what give literal life to the words they in-habit. The figures have an indefinite longevity. Writing is a form of revival, as well as new creation. Thus, Pablo Neruda preserves the voices and gestures of many generations in his *Canto General*; in her novel *Tinísima* (1992) Elena Poniatowska reconstructs, together with innumerable other revolutionary personalities between the mid-1920s and the early 1940s, the agitated life of the photographer Tina Modotti; Borges, aging and visually impaired for this world, contin-ues his walk, tapping his way through metaphysical labyrinths; Julia de Burgos arises on images from her remote New York suicide; Rubén Darío (prematurely old but continuously erotic, perpetuates himself in the youthful alter ego of *Oro de Mallorca*; and at the end of *Rayuela*, Horacio Oliveira the protagonist inadvertently complies with postmodern indeterminacy as he stands on a windowsill of the insane asylum where he's employed. Will he leap forward to his death? Will he step back to the security or dilemma of his existence? Is the question mark the ultimate form of narrative closure?

Indeterminacy, to be sure. But the hesitation is creative. Like the dynamic "graphism" that preceded him (Don Quijote), Horacio Ol-iveira in his quandary and implied defeat remains a vital, memorable figure. He persists as a presence, just as in their respective eras and styles, the errant knight and José Rubén Romero's vagabond Pito Pérez do. Pito's final resting place is the village garbage dump; but we remember him more as a backlighted silhouette framed in the arch of the village bell tower as he pulls once more on the ropes to announce his return for the next chapter of his story.

As readers we owe these creations acknowledgement, because we are vitalized by their dilemmas; and because a figure—whether lyric or narrative—is at once its author's self-projection and an echo of his or her muses. Figures are the author's closest if not always willing collaborators. They're also the reader's welcome accomplices.

2
Pérez Galdós: Mortality and the Gilded Age

Benito Pérez Galdós and Julio Cortázar—obviously enough—had little in common: historically, culturally, or stylistically. In the Spaniard's *Novelas contemporáneas* reality and symbol fit together like notches and dowels in a carefully crafted piece of Victorian furniture. By contrast in *Rayuela* (1963) anything goes. It's a flea market of modern motifs, a novel with a large number of its chapters classified as "dispensable," a story of impossible closure, an intermittent celebration of the absurd with clever juxtapositions of incompatible elements. Among its festivities is Cortázar's bitextual experiment with an involuntary collaborator.

That is, in chapter 34 the author of *Rayuela* intertwines the opening section of part 1 of Pérez Galdós's *Lo prohibido* (1884–85) and his own protagonist's negative reaction to it. The contrast gets extra emphasis with the placement of Galdós's and Cortázar's texts on alternate lines. The opening passage of *Lo prohibido* is probably the most insufferably tedious in Galdós's complete works. It's his introduction to the aristocratic and mostly psychosomatic Bueno de Guzmán family, in which the narrator praises a frivolous Andalusian uncle who is afflicted with a fear of falling and a chronic inflammation of the tear ducts. Uncle Rafael is a man memorable for his business deals, social discretion and an incomparable embroidered handkerchief collection. Horacio can't understand his girlfriend's fascination with the work (la Maga is much more romantically inclined than he is), in his opinion "a cold tasteless soup" and a stilted exposition of fermented old ideas.

Nevertheless, Galdós has to his credit an impressive group of unforgettable figures, and this passage is an inseparable part of his collective portrayal. Notwithstanding all their visible differences, he and the Argentinian share and exploit the tedium that oozes from this passage. Novelistic characters in the nineteenth century are generally more identifiable than those of later works. They stand out in relative clarity, as figures in a familiar, discernible sense, with multiple connections to their respective societies and cultures. In many Russian, North American, Western European, and Latin American works the identity of protagonists is symbolically highlighted in titles of the books they appear in: Madame Bovary, Facundo, Huckleberry Finn, the Brothers Karamazov, María, Martín Fierro, Père Goriot, Torquemada, David Copperfield, Fortunata, Anna Karenina, Dom Casmurro, and (nature as the great equalizer? the enactment of providential wrath?) Moby Dick. We remember them for their eccentricities, their sharpness of image or gesture, their power as fictional generators of circumstance and atmosphere.

We also remember many of them as infected by the *morbus romanticus*. Important characters in the works of Balzac, Dostoevsky, and Pérez Galdós progressively reveal themselves as born losers, misfit lovers, or victims in the making. In the nineteenth-century naturalistic view, individuals struggle against a kind of historical inevitability not recognized in previous eras. With romanticism, the delicate machinery of eighteenth-century thought is corroded by subjective organisms. The writer's rational compulsions give way to psychological curiosity; and—as Jacques Barzun has observed in *Classic, Romantic and Modern*, biology largely displaces physics in the Romantic artist's and writer's thought processes. A few decades later, the best novels classified as "realistic" reflect new and diverse realities, and from that diversity broader and deeper perspectives spring forth. Characters produced in those conditions are figures in the most dynamic sense. They exceed normal human dimensions. Think of Père Goriot's relationship with his two egoistic daughters; of how Prince Myshkin attracts or repels representative members of St. Petersburg society; and of the fascination that several characters in Galdós's Madrid have with Fortunata.

In referring to Romanticism's alleged victory over Neoclassicism as that of biology over mechanics, Jacques Barzun identifies the romantics' motivating force as "the individual's and the species' survival." He believes that with Romanticism western religion is transformed into "an energetic theory" that animates human beings and their natural environment.[1] Religion then becomes "an intellectual and emotional necessity," as much as a spiritual mandate. And for the same reason, the variety of realities found in the most important novels of the nineteenth century have their parallel in the multiform

religiosity of the same era. Skepticism, which is the dominant attitude in the modern novel, stimulates that variety. The perceptions
of Balzac, Dostoevsky, and Pérez Galdós are their barometer of profound intellectual changes. From Hegel to Nietzsche philosophy has
moved from logic to idealism; science from speculative thought to
applied procedure; religion from established orthodoxies to panthe-
istic mysticism; and literature from evocation (often of local customs) of the past to preoccupation (usually social) for the future.
Everything can be defined in terms of *necessity* combined with continual questioning. In his or her particular situation each protagonist asks, in effect: What am I to do about my death? That question
is their main contribution to the story.

The attempt is made in a comparative essay on Balzac and Galdós
to show in the former's work "the jubilation and optimism of a bap-
tism" in contrast to the Spaniard's "quiet and moving sorrow of a
viaticum."[2] The simplification, to say the least, is misleading. Basically and in considerable detail, the *Comédie Humaine* is a vision of
life as an incurable disease. In Galdós's case, several of his principal
and secondary characters experience—in nightmares, lost illusions,
crazy spells, or simple financial frustrations—the same psychological
inferno symbolized in the first chapter of *La Peau de chagrin* (1830).
There modern civilization is seen as a drab casino supervised by a
sinister old man who receives each customer's hat and seems to be
a guardian of the portals of Death. In that novel life fatigues and
constricts, like goatskin (*chagrin*) itself, and of course, a pun is involved: the *Nouveau Petit Larousse* lists its principal meaning as *afflic-
tion,* and gives a second definition as "*cuir grenu, en peau de chèvre ou
de mouton.*" It's the talisman accepted by Raphaël, "that power-
giving but steadily shrinking talisman," writes Victor Brombert, "in
which Balzac symbolizes the eternal dialectic of desire and death."[3]
As each wish is fulfilled the goatskin shrinks a little more, a persistent reminder that life is a diminishing process and an unending
succession of disappointments.

Los episodios nacionales: A Tragicomic View of History

In his *Novelas contemporáneas* Galdós fills out and humanizes the
historical panorama developed in the two early series of *Episodios
nacionales.* Not just in the hallucinations and fears of selected charac-

ters for whom the specter of Death appears, but in History itself. Ricardo Gullón appropriately calls attention to the general insecurity and the narrator's "light mental disturbances" in the final series of the *Episodios*. He also perceives a tragic consistency in the whole series.[4] I'm more inclined to characterize Galdós's view as tragicomic, even in the most pessimistic passages of the final series. For example: in its panorama of frivolities, its historical ironies and its political caricatures, in Galdós's steadily growing sarcasm over Spanish *cursilería* (shabby gentility).[5] For Galdós history—just as much as personal life—is tragicomic, and the final chapter of the last *Episodio* (*Cánovas*, 1912) presents in the form of a letter from the Muse of History to the narrator-protagonist this view of Spain's present and future:

"Peace is an infirmity if it represents the indolence of a race and its inability to find a practical solution to the basic needs of eating and thinking. The *ridiculous era* I told you about will unfold over long years of passivity, of slow paralysis that will carry you all to consumption and death."[6]

Mariclío (the Muse) adds that Spain will end up handing over to the Holy Mother's Church "public education, wealth, civic power, and even national independence," that only some kind of revolution will lift the nation out of its lethargy, and that meanwhile she—the restless Muse of History—will fall asleep out of boredom. Thus spoke the Hispanic Zarathustra, the tired storyteller and prophet, in 1912. Many times before then, in a variety of circumstances, the author had expressed the same premonitions. As Robert Ricard points out in his analysis of the *Episodio Prim* (1906) Galdós's historical point of view ranged between two extremes—tragic and farcical. An ambiguity between two other extremes—logical and irrational seems to be implied. Ricard observes that through his historian Santiuste the novelist wants to demonstrate in the context of his own time Don Quijote's concept, *la razón de la sinrazón* ("the logic of the irrational").[7] Juan Santiuste has the unequivocal nickname "Confucius" and is the author of a scattershot *Historia lógico-natural de los españoles de ambos mundos en el siglo XIX* ("Logical-Natural History of the Spaniards of Both Worlds in the Nineteenth Century"). "My history," writes Santiuste unfettered by modesty, "is not of vulgar reality but of the noble kind that divine Principle instills in human Logic. I write in behalf of the Universe, of the elevated spirits in whom total thought resides." (*OC* 3:619) Santiuste's treatise and the fuzzy conclusion toward which it leads correspond roughly to Maxi Rubín's last thoughts in the next-to-last chapter of *Fortunata y Jacinta* (1886–87)—also significantly titled "*La razón de la sinrazón*—that is, to "the furor of logic" that Maxi experiences. The unbalanced historian and the alternately rational and crazy philosopher enact similar spiritual levitations, a comic mixture of Hegelian logic and quixotic fantasy. In work after work—*Episodios* and *Novelas contemporáneas* —Galdós offers his spectacle of social and historical illusions, of characters blind to reality and unable to comprehend their circumstances. The political shams complicated by military interventions distort and aggravate Spain's basic problems. The "noble" reality expounded by Santiuste belongs to an imaginary world. The everyday "vulgar" kind he deplores is society's fate: a growing civic paralysis, restoration of a decadent monarchy, bureaucratic greed, extravagant pretensions.

The *Episodios nacionales* are the work of an angry witness, an ironic contrast between people's true nature and their desires. They constitute a generic hybrid of novel, diary, and journalism and, accordingly, are of vital interest to serious readers of Spanish history. They lack the profundity of the best nineteenth-century novels, but the first and second series of them (published between 1873 and 1879) are instrumental and very useful as a prelude to the *Novelas contemporáneas*. The *Episodios*, then, have two functions: (1) as the organized notes of a historically organized novelist and (2) as notebooks of his civic and social preoccupations. Galdós was an enthusiast but not a philosopher of history. From his first works to the last his historical approach is genealogical and personal; its focus is on the streets, fashions, and living rooms of Madrid directly familiar to him. He saw society as simultaneous development and deterioration of Spanish customs. Everything happened in families, in labyrinthine households, in dreams and nightmares of limited horizons. But lights and shadows, like the emotions, were intense. Intimate lives, intimate deaths.

PERSPECTIVES ON DEATH

As a citizen and amateur psychiatrist of nineteenth-century Spain, Galdós interpreted death in three basic ways: (1) as a consequence of natural selection; (2) as a degenerative process; (3) as a spiritual dénouement.

Natural Selection. Galdosian naturalism, oblique but always present, is notable in several characters. "Everything that has fulfilled its function disappears," states Máximo Manso (*El amigo Manso,* 1882) as he senses the imminence of his own disappearance. (*OC* 4:1289) And he adds, in retrospect, "My tranquility gave me the impression that I no longer existed as a man." José Ido del Sagrario, the delirious prophet and literary theorist in *El doctor Centeno* (1883) declares on the occasion of Alejandro Miquis' death: "the world eliminates and discards those who are no longer useful to it." (*OC* 4:1448) Frasquito Ponte, doña Paca's faithful friend in *Misericordia* (1897) ends up as another disposable person: an anachronistic gentleman who tries to conceal his miserable condition (as he hides his threadbare suit the year-round under a summer overcoat) with dreams of possible good fortune. His downfall is represented by two physical falls: the first, especially undignified one, from his horse; the second, definitive and mortal, down the whole staircase in Doña Paca's house. These are people, like the degraded aristocrat Rafael del Aguila in *Torquemada en la cruz* (1893) and *Torquemada en el purgatorio* (1894), who no longer have a place in the bourgeois world of Spain in the 1870s and 1880s. Three deaths and a suicide determined—it seemed—by the rough social conditions of the era. As a reader of Herbert Spencer, Charles Darwin, and Emile Zola, Galdós applied the concepts of natural selection and "struggle for life" to human society, not with scientific precision but in a symbolic dimension. Madrid then, like Puccini's Paris in *La Bohème,* was a hard place for impoverished poets, artists, and nobles, and Galdós was well aware of his role as witness of a society that resisted all forms of innovation except materialistic ones in the context of social competitivenes.

A Degenerative Process. This phenomenon is frequently referred to in commentaries on *La desheredada* (1881) and *Lo prohibido* (1884–85). *Lo prohibido* is a virtual encyclopedia of psycho-physical disorders caused by a morbid attraction to luxury (*Radix malorum cupiditas est*). Walter T. Pattison observes that that the whole Bueno de Guzmán family dreams of pleasures that only money can bring, and because of the characters' waste and greed, the money they're able to acquire is never enough.[8] The basic malady in *Lo prohibido,* as in the work immediately preceding it (*La de Bringas,* 1884) and in the later four-volume *Torquemada* series (1889–95) is materialism in the garbs of fashion. Pattison refers to Galdós view of it as "mitigated naturalism." I see it more as metaphorical naturalism. The author repeatedly uses biological or physiological imagery to imply a character's deterioration as a person or a family's degradation. Emile Zola, a close adherent to Claude Bernard's determinism, believes that all phenomena (effects) have specific, recognizable causes. In his view the novelist is a synthesis of the observer and the experimentalist, and that his task is to submit characters to a "series of tests."[9] Well in advance of the structuralist concept, he stresses that experimental science should not concern itself with the *why* of things; its purpose is to show the *how.*"[10]

For his part, Galdós the concerned citizen, "the liberal crusader" in H. Chonon Berkowitz's phrase, the spiritual father of modern Spain, insisted always on an artistic balance between the stylistic *how* and the psychological *why*. In accordance with Ortega y Gasset's later contention in *España invertebrada* (1921) and Américo Castro's view in *La realidad histórica de España* (1948), Galdós gives us a naturalism in reverse, in which people's individual wills and whims determine the conditions in which they and those around them live. Circumstances are mirrors of the persons who consciously or unconsciously create them. He sees usury, bureaucracy, Franco-Hispanic fashions, family, and social patriarchy, and visible or hidden hunger as *effects*, secondary circumstances: the product of a multiple, tenaciously Spanish personality, the result of desires, dreams, and rationalizations often incompatible with reality.

Consider a few examples. The death of Pepe Carrillo, Eloísa's husband in *Lo prohibido*, foreshadows that of Tolstoy's protagonist in "The Death of Ivan Ilyich" (1886). In each case the end is a bizarre poem of pain and screaming. Carrillo's cries are "the expression of an endangered, wounded animal, devoid of ideas or anything else that distinguishes man from beast." (*OC* 4:1756) His wife's later death is still worse. Eloísa's face at the time is described by the narrator (who is also her ex-lover) as an "enormous pumpkin." In its moribund state the repugnant visage replaces the character's former dazzling beauty with "all humanity's ironies." (*OC* 4: 1829) Eloísa and to a lesser extent her husband, had practiced a life of maximum social pretension—so extreme that the only possible outcome was failure and death. She had, as the popular saying goes, "mucha cara," and symbolically died with her face grotesquely swollen. Rafael, an uncle of the narrator, reviews at the beginning of *Lo prohibido* several lives in the strange Bueno de Guzmán family. One of them, José María's uncle, had his own pantheon built and decreed in his will that all the poor children who died in Ronda (several of whom were his own) be buried around it; another, the narrator's grandfather, was thought to have the habit of "wrapping himself in a shroud and walking the streets of Ronda at night" to frighten the inhabitants. (*OC* 4:1678) Raimundo, Rafael's son, had "an astounding talent for uselessness." In sum, all prominent members of the family are exemplars of failure.

The Spiritual Outcome. Of course death—for the uncomprehending as well as the most perceptive—is the deepest mystery. Máximo Manso is obsessed with it. He thinks of it as the basic and final form of nonexistence: nonbeing construed by a creator (such as a novelist would offer). Manso spiritualizes life, while Manolo Peña (his disciple) materializes it. Each in his way senses the incompatibility between spirit and matter, which in effect could be called the essence of death. By contrast, Francisco de Bringas doesn't *think* about death, but he lives, breathes, and expresses it every day. His progressive blindness is the metaphor of his incomprehension. In the creation of his masterpiece he experiences "artistic spasms" that fail to compensate for his social, economic, and cultural problems. His money doesn't circulate; his limited vision excludes the future, as well as reality. His scruffy cenotaph is the perfect figure and function of his spiritually miserable existence. It's a partly gothic, partly baroque, partly romantic communion of the living and the dead, represented by the varicolored snips and ringlets of their hair. Galdós's painstakingly detailed description of this artistic and architectural wonder (*La de Bringas* begins with the author's puzzled fascination: "*Era aquello . . . , cómo lo diré yo?*"). His creation is an ironic monument to the social disease of *cursilería*. Significantly, immediately after his presentation of the cenotaph, the novelist gives us an analogous figure, the first of several descriptions of the Royal Palace's interior. The Bringas family has an apartment there, a fringe benefit for Don Francisco as a minor government official. Significantly again, the family is forced to vacate the premises when, in September 1868, the reign of Queen Isabel II comes to an abrupt end. The Bringas family witnesses the downfall of a decadent monarchy and faces the prospect of life in a new, unproductive middle-class society.

If the Bringas family was the prose of the era, Fortunata was the poetry. For the same reason she resists death more effectively. As

José Schraibman indicates, she is the most active dreamer in *Fortu-nata y Jacinta*; nine of the twenty-three dreams in the novel are hers.[11] "Dying fulfills a law of harmony," remarks Juan Pablo Rubín in the presence of several "ladies of equivocal morals." (*OC* 5:307); and Fortunata herself—his sister-in-law—seems to demonstrate the validity of that law (partly Christian, partly Darwinian) of acceptable extinction. She is one of few Galdosian characters to die in peace with her/himself. Her last words (*"Soy angel . . . yo también . . . , mona del Cielo"*) intone satisfaction and the conviction of having achieved in full freedom her goal as woman and mother. Guillermina Pacheco insists that she forgive her lover, Juanito de Santa Cruz. But, despite Guillermina's objections, she holds tenaciously to the idea that she (Fortunata) and not Jacinta has been Juanito's true wife. Significantly, on the threshold of death, for most people the occasion for maximum concessions to religion and social discretion, for Fortunata it's the time to reaffirm her will. She won't concede to society her claim as wife, nor to religion any *mea culpa*. She's "an angel," no less; that is, an agent of unconditional love, and a figurative "monkey from Heaven"; that is, an uncorrupted creature and only mother possible of the figurative baby monkey, *"mono del Cielo"*: a necessary contrast between the mother-and-son couple as she sees herself and her baby, and the crueler societal view expressed by her mother-in-law Doña Lupe in the words *pájara mala* ("bad bird") and *pollo* ("chicken").

THREE EXEMPLARY VICTIMS

Galdós was well aware that life for a woman in his time was especially hard, as his characters Isidora Rufete, Mauricia la Dura, and Tristana, among others, reflect it. He found in society the nucleus of all the injustices suffered by women. Madrid is presented as an extended family of victims and victimizers, vividly portrayed in the closing years of an era. The implicit naturalism of the *Novelas con-temporáneas* shows the individual's ironic ineptitude (male as well as female) in a culture founded on the tradition of individualism but now losing itself in a (tarnished) gilded age. That ineptitude is colored by a peculiar view of death that is detected and skillfully described by the author. His women are in many cases more vital and portrayed in greater psychological depth than his men; but the men usually express (and enact) a greater preoccupation with human mortality.

Three characters with fascinating weaknesses deserve special attention for the ways in which they anticipate death: 1) Fortunata's husband Maxi Rubín, for his continuous infirmity (physical, nervous, and mental); 2) Ramón Villamil (in *Miau*), the most complete victim of his own family, political, and social situation; 3) Francisco de Torquemada, transformed from minor to major parasite on Spanish society. The first is still alive at the end of *Fortunata y Jaccinta* but life has left him no options; he's isolated from family and friends, and confined to an insane asylum. The second, Villamil, is almost systematically humbled and frustrated and opts for suicide. Torquemada, the third, is the most explicit in his concern for the other world, not in the context perceived by Antonio Sánchez Barbudo (i.e., in anticipation of Miguel de Unamuno's existential anguish) but much more precisely as an economic animal in search of the ultimate investment.[12] "Living," for Torquemada, means the unending accumulation of wealth.

Maxi Rubín dies because he fails to achieve complete manhood. His pathological condition is a metaphor of his weak character. He dies deprived of love, which was his only possible salvation. In the last chapter Fortunata offers him *her* love, but only on the condition that he first kill her rival Aurora and Juanito Santa Cruz, Fortunata's former lover and father of their natural child. Combined with her contribution of money to buy a pistol, the offer is of course preposterous, since no such amorous relationship can materialize. Their real separation has been in effect since their wedding night. Fortunata exists as a double enigma: the elusive *"eterno femenino,"* and a subliminal symbol of Spain on the threshold of modernity. For his part, Maximiliano Rubín is a parody of manhood, a pathetic reversal of the Don Juan legend (by contrast, Juanito de Santa Cruz is one more exacerbation of it). Poor Maxi lacks authority, physical appeal, eloquence, good health, poise. In the relative tranquility of Leganés, the insane asylum, he'll function as sporadic philosopher—not so much by vocation as by the process of elimination: he's unqualified for anything else. With a shade of cruelty comparable to that of Cervantes when he identifies himself in the prologue as "stepfather" of Don Quijote, Galdós ironically labels Maxi (part 2, chapter 2) as "the Redeemer." He has no more chance of redeeming Fortunata (i.e., for social acceptance and his own happiness) than Don Quijote had of redeeming Aldonza Lorenzo, or the deluded protagonist in Nikolai Gogol's story "Nevski Avenue," a prostitute. Maxi is more than a simple weakling; he's the reversal of masculine power, a showcase of pathological symptoms. Other unrequited lovers are partly redeemed by the poetry of their lamentations. The features of Maxi's fate are entirely prosaic: impotence, fainting spells, hallucinatory fevers, and a runny nose. Fortunata's infidelity causes him nothing but nightmares and exacerbates a progressive madness that culminates in his maxim: "Incarnation is a punishment or a test. Death is liberation and a pardon: true life, that is. The sooner it comes, the better." (*OC* 5:432)

Maxi's last words (also the last words of *Fortunata y Jacinta*): "They can't imprison my thought within walls. I live in the stars. Leave the man called Maximiliano Rubín in a palace or on a dung heap . . . ; it makes no difference." Walter Pattison compares that statement on imprisonment with a similar one by Pierre in *War and Peace*, and which Galdós marked in his copy of Tolstoy's novel.[13] But it should be noted that Tolstoy held Pierre in higher esteem than Galdós did for Maxi. Impotence is the latter's basic trait, and his late spiritual triumph is not entirely convincing.

Ramón Villamil at the end of *Miau* achieves—via suicide—a more specific kind of "liberation." However, he and Maxi are similar victims in their personal and social isolation. Both are continually afflicted by their frustrations and their premonitions of death. Villamil's suicide and Rubín's definitive enclosure in Leganés are parallel failures in a naturalistic context. Maxi's sexual impotence is the metaphor of his incapacity for everything except his "philosophy." Ramón is seen as a martyr of the bureaucratic system in which he flounders, but he's also the victim of social pretension—that of his wife Pura, and his sister-in-law Milagros, of his daughter Abelarda's nervous condition, of his son-in-law Víctor Cadalso's machinations, and of two daughters' and one grandson's epilepsy. His family is one of several portrayed by Galdós (for example, those of Rosalía de Bringas, Doña Perfecta, Eloísa de Carrillo, and Cruz de Aguila) manipulated by domineering women. In *Miau* the impoverished "three Meows" scornfully control the old "tiger" Villamil and waste what little money the family has left. "Ramón, get ready to hock your watch; our girl needs new boots." Villamil is the honorable man defeated by his predetermined personal relationships. His formula for rescuing the national economy ("Honesty, Income Tax, Customhouses, Unity") was what Spain in the 1880s needed. But those in power were not willing to accept it. Villamil's frustration slowly evolves into madness. His contract as a civil servant has permanently expired, and he replaces his prescription for economic regeneration with another for vengeance: "Death, Infamy, Curses on the Universe." (*OC* 5:679) Only his nine-year-old grandson Luisito loves him, and the child's epilepsy and nightmares directly reflect Villamil's unbearable existence. "The world rids itself of those who fail to serve it," José Ido del Sagrario had already declared in *El doctor Centeno* (*OC* 5:1448); and the world (with the efficient collaboration of the Spanish bureaucracy and his opportunistic family) easily rids itself of Ramón Villamil, who for such a long time had been mentally incubating his death in a dark room at home.

The author's culminating figure of the Spanish Gilded Age is Francisco de Torquemada, the moneylender. As his last name suggests, he has a certain affinity in the modern material world with the first and foremost of the Grand Inquisitors. Torquemada is the character who grows the most—literally—through several of Galdós's novels. Starting as the vague profile of a usurer, he swells as a personality, acquiring real estate, family, the title of marquis, political prestige, and a powerful standing in the financial world. Don Francisco is the balloon person, progressively inflated with material wealth, who after an abundant meal at the end of part 2 of the fourth and final novel of the Torquemada series (*Torquemada y San Pedro*) symbolically and torrentially vomits. Although time remains for him to settle his estate and mentally prepare for the "supreme voyage" as Father Gamborena puts it, he is terminally ill.

It should be remembered that Torquemada is not only the great Materialist always ready to sacrifice his clients. He represents an evolution that moves simultaneously toward Abundance and Death; that is, from "metaphysical" to "positivistic" usury. (*OC* 5:908) As he overcomes his simple obsession with numbers that characterizes the traditional *prestamista*—quantity as a value in itself—Don Francisco develops a financial philosophy more compatible with a "religion of the refined materiality of existence" widely practiced in several countries in the second half of the nineteenth century. His first spiritual guide is an ex-priest, José Bailón, of whose theology Torquemada understands very little. But he celebrates Bailón's favorite concept: "God is Humanity," and utilizes it as the founding principle of his greed and his actions.

Everything in Torquemada's life and person manifests itself in deterioration. His child-prodigy son who dies in the first volume (*Torquemada en la hoguera*)—Valentín the genius of abstract mathematics, in contraposition to his father the master of hard cash and solid budgets—returns to the story twice: first as a debilitated ghost, and second as a demented monster. Combined with his role as failed father is a comparable one as fiancé and husband. Fidela, at the end of *Torquemada en la cruz*, marries the great Miser—not because she wants to, but on the decision of her sister Cruz (the name here being a symbol of society). The wedding takes place (once again, a symbol) on an extra-hot summer day of San Santiago, patron saint of Spain (*OC* 5:1011), and represents the union of a losing aristocracy with a triumphant bourgeoisie. Coincidentally Fidela, having taken as a remedy for the heat a glass of *agraz* (a bitter refreshment concocted from unripe grapes) suffers an ominously high fever; and Torquemada, after plying himself with the champagne that he had to pay for anyway and still reeking of the onions he'd eaten the night before, disrupts the luncheon party with vulgar language and barbaric laughter. Still another symbol is developed in the role of Rafael del Aguila, Cruz's and Fidela's brother, who sees Fidela's marriage to Torquemada as the prelude to her death. His own suicide at the end of *Torquemada en el purgatorio* expresses not only diillusionment with his sister's sacrifice, but also the conviction that his whole social class is on the threshold of extinction.

Fidela's death in *Torquemada y San Pedro* causes Francisco's second epileptic seizure (*OC* 5:1146), similar to the one he experienced when his son died. When Fidela dies the physical decline of the Marqués de San Eloy accelerates in a series of dyspeptic episodes. José Donoso, his progressive counselor, and Father Gamborena, his preliminary St. Peter, cannot help or save him. Torquemada's death will be comparable to a failed major business deal.

Three exemplary victims. Neither Torquemada's "force and matter," nor Maxi Rubín's frail "spiritual substance," nor Ramón Villamil's persistent honesty suffice for their salvation. Torquemada, who ignores the importance of both Nature and Civilization, dies in his attempt to exist in unrestricted materiality. Maxi the Impotent dies for trying to live in a spiritual world so pure that it merges with madness. Villamil dies struggling against his family's social pretensions and the corruption of his bureaucratic colleagues. Galdós leaves each of them in his predestined solitude, recognizing in the Gilded Age that became his literary fascination the unlikelihood of a solution.

3

Octavio Paz: The Circumstances of Poetry

A poem should be equal to:
Not true

For all the history of grief
An empty doorway and a maple leaf

For love
The leaning grasses and two lights above the sea—
—Archibald MacLeish

"POET," IN OLD GREEK AS WELL AS IN OLD ENGLISH, MEANS *MAKER*, AND even though modern dictionaries classify it with a small "m" as archaic, they also give *maker* as a definition of the lyric vocation. And of course, with a capital "M" the word still means *God*. The word's duration and its providential overtones give it special significance. It's a metaphor for the power of lyric writing and casts the poet in many roles: privileged visionary, singer, inventor, representative of universal desires, believer, lover, unbeliever, adventurer, *creator*. The significance of the word as creator also stands out in the title Jorge Luis Borges gave one of his books, *El hacedor* (1960)

In 1916, the year that the founders of Dada met in Zurich, the year that Rubén Darío returned to Nicaragua scarcely in time to succumb to his final delirium, the year that Juan Ramón Jiménez simultaneously prayed and decreed that the word and what it represented be identical ("Que mi palabra sea / la cosa misma"), Vicente Huidobro (calling himself a *creationist*) declared "the poet is a little god."

Jiménez and Huidobro were telling us, in effect, that poetry functions in ways analogous to divinity and nature—a mythical concept that makes criticism difficult and theory close to impossible. In the beginning of conscious human history—reputedly after Adam and

45

Eve's experiment in Eden—was the Word. Neither André Breton's belief that words are unpremeditated acts nor Aristotle's idea that they're instruments of practical persuasion tells us where the Word comes from or what its ultimate effect might be. Nevertheless, those two inseparable questions are the poet's basic concern. From the most primitive ode to the complex music of *The Wasteland*, the poem has been the human self's most persistent form of inquiry, as well as a literary process.

Poetry is the process by which the individual imagination leads the Self to the remotest regions of the non-Self. *This* world acquires greater substance and vitality as it relates to *other* worlds. Octavio Paz was strongly aware of that connection.

The Poet and Spain

"El camino se hace al andar," wrote Antonio Machado ("The road forms as it is traveled"), long before Octavio Paz set out for Galta in *El mono gramático* (1970), his hallucinated pilgrimage through language and, at the same time, a mystic and erotic journey through a blurred landscape of India.[1] For Paz, an early disciple of the Spanish poet's in another sense (his adoption of Machado's concept of each individual's "otherness"), poetry does not form a path. Rather, it continually detours itself onto new paths. At least that is what he tells us in this testimony:

> As I began writing these pages I decided to follow literally the metaphorical title of the collection they appear in, *The Paths of Creation*, and to write, trace a text that would form a path and could be read and followed as such. As I was writing the road to Galta faded away and I lost myself in its twists and turns. Repeatedly I tried to get back to the beginning. But instead of progressing, the text turned on itself. Is destruction actually creation? I don't know; but I do know creation is not destruction. At each turn the text turned into another, at the same time a translation and transposition: a spiral of repetitions and reiterations that have turned out to be a rejection of writing as a path.[2]

At first sight it seems that Paz was acting as spokesman for the structuralist mode of the time (circa 1970), but actually he was expressing a critical view that he consistently held: language—not nationality—is the true foundation of a literature. Society and culture survive on the strength of what they speak and write, out of which an infinity of styles emerges. A literature acquires strength and form only in the measure that it acquires a *critical awareness*. Critical awareness, in turn, engenders a new sensibility, new perspectives, new values: Rubén Darío in his generation, Jorge Luis Borges in his, Octavio Paz in his, etc.

In the prologue to the essays of *Puertas al campo* (1966) Paz reminds his readers that as recently as forty years before (i.e., the 1920s) the Mexican intelligentsia viewed the world through European—mainly French—eyes, adding: "French influence has never seemed to me a sin." Further on he refers to "the great fragment of our being called Spain" and "the impossibility of a dialogue" with Spaniards, even though Mexicans' relationship with them "has always oscillated between absolute solidarity and an indifference no less absolute."[3]

On three historic occasions (Napoleon's occupation of Spain in 1808; the Spanish-American War of 1898, and the Spanish Civil War of 1936 to 1939) "absolute solidarity" prevailed. Especially during and after the civil war. "On July 19, 1936," said Paz in a 1951 speech in Paris, "the Spanish people entered history as in a miraculous explosion of well-being."[4] The "explosion" also had evident effects on Paz's subsequent writing.

The principal poets born in Hispanic America before 1915 share a vital experience: their active relationship with Spain. First was Rubén Darío. Then came Alfonso Reyes, César Vallejo, Gabriela Mistral, Vicente Huidobro, Pablo Neruda, and Octavio Paz. Each of them found attractions, relationships, and affinities that transcended intellectual curiosity. Even Jorge Luis Borges, who consistently overlooked Spanish writers after the era of Cervantes, Quevedo, and Gracián, spent the first phase of his youthful *ultraísmo* in the *madre patria*, stimulated by his conversations with Rafael Cansinos Assens between 1919 and 1921.

Of all those poets probably Paz formed the strongest spiritual bond between Spain and Hispanic America. The first phase of his literary initiation was in 1937 and 1938, in the revolutionary, fratricidal, and civil turbulence of Spain's greatest war.[5] But there was an important premonition—and one could say a prevision—of the war in the friendship that Paz formed with a schoolmate in Mexico City in 1929. The friend's name was José Bosch, a Catalonian who participated actively in the student protests and strikes in support of José

Vasconcelos' presidential campaign that year. Because of those activities he was arrested and deported (from the port of Veracruz) in 1930.

Time passed and nothing was known about Bosch until his name as a victim on the Aragon front appeared in a Mexican newspaper. On the basis of that report Paz wrote his elegy ("You died comrade,/ in the world's burning dawn"). A few months later, in 1937 or early 1938, Paz was in Barcelona, at a meeting of the Sociedad de Amigos de México. He was asked to read his elegy to the fallen comrade and two or three other poems. Then, near the beginning of his reading—with appropriate funereal respect—he noticed the undeniable presence of José Bosch in a first-row seat. In 1929 Bosch had introduced his Mexican friend to anarchistic works by Kropotkin, Ferrer, Proudhon, and others. Now, the day after the Barcelona meeting, he and Paz would see each other and speak for the last time. Since then nothing was heard of Bosch.

I've referred to this friendship because it anticipates in a way Paz's literary career, and his view of history. *"El ardiente amanecer del mundo"* of his elegy, which for so many of the Civil War's participants was a hopeful metaphor for Spain's future, would soon degenerate into a bloody nightmare. The solidarity with which it began crumbled in internal struggles among liberals, anarchists, and communists. Against the fascist monolith formed by General Franco, unity disintegrated.

By 1939 Spain was a graveyard of hopes. By August 1945, World War II was over, but the only two nuclear bombs used in combat in the twentieth century had obliterated two Japanese cities and—besides—permanently mutilated the future. In 1956, in the epilogue to the first edition of *El arco y la lira* (Mexico City: Fondo de Cultura Económica, 1956, 263) Paz observes: "Historical consciousness, ultimately, has shown itself to be tragic consciousness; the present no longer projects itself into the future. Man is immersed in something final and definitive which has totally affected his present, his past and his future. Accordingly, the poet discovers tragedy—and with it, his country and the world."

His statement carries an echo of Miguel de Unamuno's basic concern: the idea that history develops forms of shared desperation, a sense of *"quiero-y-no puedo"* enunciated by poets and prophets and experienced by all, a tragic sense of life in Unamuno's own phrase. In the epilogue to the second edition (1967) of Paz's above-mentioned work (*"Los signos en rotación"*) the dilemma intensifies. Now "history makes no sense," because "our time excludes from history an imaginable or comprehensible future."

And that seems to be the case. Since 1945 "the present does not project itself into a future." Spain's war and the multination conflagration that followed it expressed an epilogue more than a prologue, for historians as much as for poets. Especially for Octavio Paz. It was in that twilight atmosphere of growing indeterminacy and confusion, with its exclusion from history of "an imaginable or comprehensible future," that he wrote his major poems and essays.

At this point a critical parenthesis regarding Spain's two principal thinkers of the twentieth century (Unamuno and Ortega y Gasset) might be useful. Unamuno is admirable for several reasons, but especially for his dramatic intensity: the way he embodied and expressed his struggle to believe amid his premonitions, his tragic feeling, his fateful yet inspiring *situation.* For the same reason one can accept Ortega's basic "perspectivist" idea that readers and writers should concentrate primarily on their creative "circumstances" (*"Yo soy yo y mi circunstancia"*) then, secondarily, on their works. We are interested not so much in what "happens" in *Don Quijote, Leaves of Grass, The Magic Mountain,* and *A Hundred Years of Solitude,* as in what (most literally and completely) *transpires* (i.e., breathes) in those works—in what Cervantes, Whitman, Mann, and García Márquez let us see of the grime, the turbulence, and the bliss of their respective existences. They share with us the time—or, rather, times—in which they live. The circumstantial reader—and that is what the critic needs always to be—knows that abstract thought, autonomous texts, and self-reflections are worth nothing *in themselves.* Every object depends on a subject, and vice versa. Reason, as Ortega also reminds us, is "vital." Emotion creates realities; and reality, emotions. Unamuno and Ortega together have repeatedly shown us that. But after Franco's military uprising in July 1936, Ortega seemed to lose his political awareness and opts for silence on the acceleration of the same totalitarianism he saw so clearly as a threat in *Revolt of the Masses* (1929). In retrospect, we should probably recognize that it was more a case of loss of vision than a surrender of principle. The sensitive philosopher was apparently not—to use his own phrase—*"a la altura de los tiempos."* It was as if his eyes were looking without assistance from the rest of his being.[6]

Nevertheless, Ortega continues to be an important stimulus for

Hispanic Americans to increase their historical awareness. Basically (though without ever saying so), he shared Unamuno's tragic sense. Octavio Paz sums up the issue in terms of a loss of vision and hope:

> A loss of the image of the future, said Ortega y Gasset, also implies a mutilation of the past. That's the way it is: all that once seemed to be full of meaning now appears before us as a series of efforts and creations devoid of meaning. The loss of significance affects both parts of the sphere—life and death: death has the sense that living gives it; and the ultimate significance of life is found in death. Technology can tell us nothing about this. Its philosophical virtue consists, we could say, in its elimination of philosophy. ("Los signos en rotación," epilogue to *El arco y la lira*.)[7]

Actually, Unamuno's basically religious "tragic sense of life"— which Paz extends to a tragic consciousness of new political, intellectual, and artistic dimensions—anticipated that same "loss of the image of the future." Concepts of life and death (i.e., life versus death, and death versus life) give way to technological solutions, nonphilosophy, computer-browsing, and genetic experimentation. In Paz's view the relationship between the individual and the world has been distorted. "Vision" is missing. The world loses its varied images of identity and becomes a "homogeneous space" to be exploited by ever-expanding technologies. Consequently, curiosity about *how* to do things progressively diminishes concern over *why* we do them. The evolution of Paz's own poetry seems to reflect the movement toward "homogeneous space." Compare, for example, *Piedra de sol* (1957) with *Blanco*, published ten years later. In the former, experience in the context of history (Mexican, Spanish, and universal) is alternately tender and violent. Love, war, and personal and collective memory complement one another in a vision that is both realistic and romantic. In *Blanco*, by contrast, history is practically forgotten, and the author's main effort is a clarification of the poem as sufficient reality in itself—a multiple, interchangeable one that can be read in various sequences and combinations. In the strict sense *Blanco* is not a creation, but the hallucinating spectacle of a poem in the process of creation. Accordingly, the fleeting allusions to organic life ("the land is a powdery language"; "the word greens"; "you are naked / like a syllable") highlight the metaphysical nature of the text. As Pere Gimferrer has noted, "the elements of a reality external to the poem that appear in it . . . are intended to emphasize the textual data as such, so that their function is the exact opposite of that usually undertaken by the metaphor, the metonym, or even the objective correlative."[8] Thus, things and beings are signs of language rather than vice versa. At first glance this creative dematerialization seems to be one more concession to technology: since we can't find out the *why*, let's entertain ourselves with the *how*, the means, as Marshall McLuhan thought, can become the message. In later poems Paz himself fulfills part of the prophesy expressed in "*Los signos en rotación.*" He's telling us that more and more we inhabit "a homogeneous space," and that the basic themes of poetry are silence, the void, dispersion, and oblivion. Will the blank page end up as a device for erasing history, love relationships, and desire?

Probably not. Although much of his later poetry lacks historical references, it's rich in a vital intimacy. Desire and the intensity of inner experience enhance its beauty and free it from the obligation of material reference:

Espiral de los ecos, el poema
es aire que se esculpe y se disipa,
fugaz alegoría de los nombres
verdaderos

("Spiral of echoes, the poem
is air that sculpts and fades,
a fleeting allegory of true
names")

These lines appear near the end of *Pasado en claro* (1974) Octavio Paz, *Pasado en claro* in *Obras Completas,* vol. 12 (Mexico City: Fondo de Cultura Económica, 2004), an extensive poem of evocations in which the author's recollections merge with allusions to his present creative experience.

It was always evident that Paz loved oxymorons: "the present is perpetual," "stillness in motion," "live ruins in a world of the living dead," etc. And possibly his tendency to think (or to see and hear things) in the form of opposites was a factor in his progressive withdrawal from historical circumstance, and his preference for the Word over Reality. It may also have incited him to deemphasize his underlying concern for the Mexican and Hispanic worlds in favor of the illuminations he received from the meditative Asian—especially Indian—cultures. In general, his perspective moved from a concept of *unity,* or of human beings joined in their shared feeling of solitude (in *El laberinto de la soledad,* still considered his classic essay; and *Piedra de sol,* for many readers his finest poem) toward the other concept of *dispersion* (*Blanco,* the "circulatory poem" with the revealing subtitle *"Para la desorientación general,"* *El mono gramático,* and *Arbol adentro*). In his literary criticism Paz points out the same trajectory in the language: when the Spanish language spread to the Americas it underwent extensive diversifications, particularly in literature. In the following excerpt from a 1976 lecture (*"Alrededores de la literatura hispanoamericana"*) Ortega y Gasset's idea of the importance of individual perspectives is evident:[9]

> A literary work is the result of diverse circumstances combined in unforeseeable ways: the writer's character, biography, readings, environment, and other accidents. Similar circumstances assimilated by different temperaments produce works averse to each other, or at least dissimilar. The same occurs with religion and philosophy, or the concepts that each person has of life here or in the other world. Jorge Guillén and José Gorstiza have undeniable affinities in their sensibilities and choice of readings (for example, Valéry), but those affinities diverge and express themselves in contrary visions: the same great wave of being that raises up the Spaniard overwhelms and buries the Mexican. The same verbal transparency traces, with similar sharpness, the two opposing monosyllables: Yes and No.

As a poet-thinker who didn't forget his youthful readings (prominent among them, Pérez Galdós' *Episodios nacionales*) Octavio Paz progressively defined himself in his poems and essays. That is, he developed culturally through his contacts with other cultures: in chronological order: Spanish, North American, French, Indian, or Hindu. Earlier in this chapter I referred to the fundamental importance of the Spanish Civil War in Paz's view of history; and it should be remembered how the best of Spain was reborn, during that war, in the New World. Lázaro Cárdenas, president of Mexico at the time, and the Mexican intelligentsia were strongly stimulated by the ideological undercurrents of the conflict. For Paz an important historical parallel between Spain and Hispanic America emerges from the early nineteenth-century wars of independence. He refers to the rebellions and revolutions that have "attempted to break with a suffocating past and [simultaneously] to form new political and social structures."[10] "Total support," first, for a democratic Spain against General Franco's nationalist uprising and, second, for the Spanish exiles and their cultural participation in the Americas. Spain for its part discovered—in the nineteenth century and again between 1936 and 1939—"its other historical dimension: not European but His-panic American." The relationship between Spain and America un-dergoes, he thinks, moves from *Acknowledgement* (resulting from the discovery and conquests in the sixteenth century) to *Disassociation* (when, towards the end of the eighteenth century, Spanish Ameri-cans begin to ignore their Spanish heritage in favor of French cul-ture and North American politics; in other words, their assimilation of "modernity"), and then to *Rediscovery* (the Spanish Civil War, its complex antecedents and repercussions, and certain affinities to the Mexican Revolution). Most of his essay ("México y los poetas del exi-lio español") deals with the experience of Spanish poets who began arriving in Mexico in 1938 and 1939 and little by little were Mexican-ized: Enrique Díez Canedo, Emilio Prados, Juan Gil-Albert, León Felipe, José Moreno Villa, Luis Cernuda, Manuel Altologuirre. Of his arrival in Veracruz Gil Albert recorded these impressions:

> The coast there, more than anywhere else, is deceptive, unreal, ap-pealing: with lips. Behind it is Mexico, inward and higher up; entering that infinity that awaits us has its risks; it is, to put it boldly, fatal. . . . Mexican experience is on a transcendent level. Infinity awaits the ob-server of its high plateau; infinity combined with the anxious sensation of a limit, that man's earth ends there and all that frozen, silvery and remote luminosity that glows in the surroundings is suddenly the abyss, the inhuman or superhuman region. . . . There's a feeling that the earth has closed in all around, that this is the true *finis terrae* and that from an infinite balcony we watch the movement of magnificent clouds along inaccessible routes.[11]

For Octavio Paz the *Rediscovery* (American-Spanish and Spanish-American) began in a dynamic sense in 1937: the year he left home, the university and his native city; the year he married his compatriot, the writer Elena Garro, who accompanied him to war-torn Spain—where his education began anew, his intellectual *rite of passage*, so to speak. "Spain taught me the meaning of the word *fraternity*," he told Rita Guibert.[12]

One imagines that the Spanish experience and the spirit of soli-darity that emerged from it also vitalized his readings of Cervantes, Antonio Machado, Unamuno, Ortega y Gasset, Pérez Galdós, and Jorge Guillén. Cervantes, especially, helped him formulate his the-ory of analogy and irony developed in *Los hijos del limo* (1974), for the first modern ironist was Cervantes: Cervantes discovered the contradiction between the visible world and the hidden (or sub- or ultra-) world that Dante—despite locating seven delinquent popes in the *Inferno* section of his *Divina Commedia*—perceives in terms of human progress toward individual salvation and collective harmony. Machado taught him "the basic Heterogeneity of being" or "the incurable *otherness* suffered by each *one* of us."[13] Unamuno showed him the significance of the individual's "intra-history": of *being* or becoming history at the same time as *existing in* history and of "the tragic sense of life" in individuals and peoples. And Ortega y Gasset—who systematically ignored the cultural importance of Hispanic America—helped him define Mexico's and other Hispanic-American countries' historical circumstances.[14] Pérez Galdós, whose *Episodios nacionales* of the second series Paz as a boy read in his grandfather's library, introduced him to the theme of the Two Spains impersonated by two characters, Salvador Monsalud (an exemplary liberal) and his half brother Carlos Garrote (a militant Carlist conservative), whom Paz saw as complementary in the enactment of their respective fanaticisms. Last but not least came the poetry of Jorge Guillén, who experienced ecstatic epiphanies:

Todo está concentrado	("All is concentrated,
Por siglos de raíz	By centuries rooted
Dentro de este minuto,	Within this minute,
Eterno para mí.	Eternal for me")

Guillén gave him examples of the plenitude of being reserved for the best poets and the best poems, and the demonstration that the latter—with visions like the passage from *"Más allá"* just quoted—are fertile seeds for other poems.

POETRY AND HISTORY

In 1991 President Luis Alberto Lacalle of Uruguay remarked that in the late twentieth century there had been a general devaluation of ideology in political life. In his view pragmatism and "skilful administration" had diminished the importance of the whole range of ideological programs from revolutionary socialism to right-wing reaction.[15] Could a parallel be made between that tendency in politics and a similar one in literary criticism and theory of the same period? The complex heritage of structuralism and its various bifurcations (postmodernism, poststructuralism, deconstruction, reader-response criticism, analysis of "readerly" and "writerly" texts, etc.) demanded meticulous pragmatic readings based on the *how* of a text more than the *what*. Octavio Paz himself seems to have been influenced by the trend, and in much of his poetry from *Blanco* (1967) to *Arbol adentro* (1987) he tells us how he creates his compositions as he writes them.

Nevertheless Paz preserves, in discreet measure, his immunity. His poetic work is a free zone in which fleeting images and surprises still take refuge. Indeed, poetry in general is written and read in that zone, precariously propped between everyday reality and the individual's historical consciousness. Possibly poets are less restricted and less theoretically victimized by preceding works in the genre than novelists are by theirs. Accordingly, poems often materialize as borderless spaces in which the relationship between reality and history is increasingly ambiguous. For the same reason, poets are the freest but also the least comfortable of writers.

A good book is always something more (and different) than what it seems to be. The basic value of important or "great" works is the paradox of *being* and *not being* something at the same time. *Don Quijote* is and is not a chivalric novel; *Cien años de soledad* is a narrative the realities and imaginations of which are contradictory, but at the same time complementary; in *Cantos de vida y esperanza* the esthetic exuberance celebrated by Darío is transfigured by the anxieties he suffers. Think also of *El arco y la lira*, Octavio Paz's essay on poetry that is not limited to the classification essay-on-poetry. The last of its subtitles places us on a status of alert: "Poetry and History." What does it deal with? A dichotomy? Or an affinity?

The reader of *El arco y la lira* encounters the same dilemma as its writer. Poetry—the ostensibly pure art of rhythmic composition by means of words—is an operation that cannot be seriously undertaken or analyzed without taking into account many factors that are not poetic. Of these, history is my greatest concern now. I believe that the essential part of reading and writing history is a consciousness of its progressive complication. The complication often appears to encompass movements toward chaos, but Jeremy Campbell in an important essay on the functions of information sees it rather as enrichment: "History is not a record of things unraveling, descending into chaos, but of new types of order and a richer store of information. As it moves through centuries and millennia, history is a chronicle of novelty—new structures, new organisms, new civilizations, new ideas. Information, which is a measure of novelty, increases rather than diminishes with the passage of the years."[16]

In what follows we'll see how Paz struggles by means of words, in both verse and prose to decipher that growing monster—Information ("signos en rotación") and its attendant new discoveries that lead to new mysteries. Undeniably, cumulative Information is the protean substance of our era.

A View of Modernity

El arco y la lira, Paz's most lyrical book in prose, is a *theory* of poetry in the context of modernity. But it's also his *experience* of poetry in the same context. Like all poets to a varying degree, the author of *El arco* reveals in his work a close relationship between experience and theory. In the twentieth century Modernity is the battleground on which that relationship asserts itself. For the same reason (and because of its built-in flexibility) modernity is a suspicious term, similar to many other words that end in *-ismo* or *-ity*, or begin with *post-*, *de-*, or *self-*. Scholars liberally sprinkle their word processors and blackboards with those prefixes and suffixes: modernity, postmodernism, deconstruction, poststructuralism, self-reflective. The age of painstaking *definition* and considered philosophical and historical allusions is past, and encroachments—some planned, some unforeseen—of the Information process have led many critics and some writers into a new age of random Interrogation.

As Paz observed in his Nobel Prize acceptance speech in 1990, modernity is "a word in search of its meaning."[17] The main significance of the modernity offered in *El arco y la lira*, *Corriente alterna*, and *Los hijos del limo* is an affinity between creation and criticism that reveals itself in all Paz's writing. He's telling us, in effect, that the modern writer strives to function simultaneously as creator and active (perceptive) reader. The modern writer, in the best instances, consistently discovers figurations of his or her subconscious and, in the process, gains irony. The romantics' basic point of view, he emphasizes in *Los hijos del limo*, was "analogy" between what's hoped for and the ideal; for the moderns it became a skeptical "irony," or quasi-comic separation of those same two elements. Here a distinction may help. In his repeated references to the process of creating poetry, Paz speaks of an ideal to pursue—not a reality to be achieved. It's a question of balance. In the last chapter of *Los hijos del limo* he places himself discreetly between passionate affirmation and cool-headed negation, between "*el sí pasional* and *el no reflexivo*," between Pablo Neruda's "volcano language" in *Canto general,* and José Gorostiza's "hard transparency" in *Muerte sin fin*: two monuments of modern poetry: the first to "loquacity," the second to "reticence."[18]

History and Personal Experience

In one of his more fertile aphorisms the Mexican comedian Mario Moreno (alias Cantínflas) once quipped, "Some great historic moments are truly momentary." For his part, Octavio Paz in "Nocturno de San Ildefonso" declared:

> *La poesía no es la verdad:*
> *es la resurrección de presencias,*
> *la historia*
> *transfigurada en la verdad del tiempo no fechado.*

> ("Poetry is not truth:
> it's the resurrection of presences,
> history
> transfigured in the truth of undated time.")[19]

The actor and the author were making the same general attempt: to accommodate history to the rhythm and dimensions of their own experience. They were also sharing an intuition: that Time, though a complete abstraction, forms a vital link between two completely organic human elements. One is collective and historical; the other is personal and poetic. Both Paz and Cantínflas were aware that the two elements are usually inseparable.

One historic event that Cantínflas may have granted was more momentous than momentary occurred on October 12, 1492, the day when—according to Argentine novelist Abel Posse—"animals and people of the jungle realms discovered Europe and the Europeans."[20] Most of the invaders, continues Posse, were lowly opportunists who "formulated their delirious visions of the moment under the title of History (for them a kind of metaphysical racetrack)," the most sacred symbol of which (the Cross) was also an instrument of torture. (p 27)

Negative as it appears, that point of view does not derive from the Black Legend. As is well known, the Black Legend was a non-Hispanic revision of the facts for a critique of Spanish despotism and the excesses of the Holy Inquisition. Posse's allusion interests us rather because it reflects a collective Hispanic-American awareness of prolonged historical disadvantage. Since the Reciprocal Discovery of 1492 Hispanic Americans have customarily viewed the uninvited colonists who followed Columbus's footsteps as the first *Others* to intervene in the destiny of their continent. *El Otro*, we should remember, is a basic four-letter word in Paz's poetry and thought. Hispanic-American history, it has often been argued, can be interpreted in terms of a genealogy that is not only dispersed but also different and virtually disconnected from the world's other histories.

Nevertheless, the genealogy finds voices as it grows. Gabriel García Márquez shows that with sometimes magical but always concrete portrayals in his expansive *Cien años de soledad*. Carlos Fuentes in his essay "El tiempo de Octavio Paz" identifies the latter symbolically as "a son of Mexico, brother of Latin America, stepson of Spain, adopted son of France, England and Italy, welcome guest in Japan and India, bastard son (as today we all are) of the United States."[21] A stepson of Spain—it could be added—in a way comparable to Don Quijote's relationship with Cervantes (who specifically identified the knight errant as his stepson). Don Quijote, in his time, and Octavio Paz in the twentieth century cross their respective social plateaus with an increasing awareness of their solitude. On the other hand, poets in their youth tend to transform their isolation (or alienation) into a search for solidarity. Combined with the idealistic and romantic appeal that the Spanish Civil War held for young men of several nationalities in their twenties, that feeling incited Paz to leave Mexico for the first time. "In 1937 I left at the same time my home, my university studies and Mexico City. It was my first departure."[22]

The Spanish Civil War was, clearly, his rite of passage, the shared experience that would stimulate in his imagination a stormy marriage of poetry and history. The idea that history and poetry are structurally circular is expressed in many of his poems, especially *Piedra de sol* (Mexico City: Tezontle, 1957, and in *La estación videnta*

(Mexico City: Fondo de Cultura Económica, 1958) which begins and ends with the same five-and-a-half lines:

un sauce de crystal, un chopo de agua,	("a crystalline willow, a water
un alto surtidor que el viento arquea,	poplar, a high fountain, aerially
un árbol bien plantado mas danzante,	arched,
un caminar de río que se curva,	a well-rooted tree, yet dancing,
avanza, retrocede, da un rodeo	a river-flow that curves,
y llega siempre:	advances, backs up, loops around
	and keeps arriving:")

Notice also that the first and last stanzas both end punctuated by a colon, the clearest sign of indefinite continuation.

"We are an extreme of the West."

As poet and thinker Paz often uses dichotomies. The uniqueness of his vision is complemented by the "otherness" of his thought, due in large part to his custom of simultaneously writing and reading his texts. He senses that opposites provide balance: the present is "perpetual;" oriental "conjunctions" invite comparison with occidental "disjunctions;" poetry of communion leads to poetry of solitude; and in implicit agreement with Freud as read by Norman O. Brown in *Life against Death* (1959), Paz recalls the duality of the sun and gold with excrement. The contraposition of sun and its metaphor (gold) with excrement is a paradox: i.e., high value vs. worthlessness, opposed yet fused and inseparable. The poet finds in that relationship a curious parallel with another, pointedly corporeal, duality. That is, in his prologue (1968) to A. Jiménez's best-selling *Nueva picardía mexicana* he quotes Francisco de Quevedo's euphonious if politically incorrect verses, "*La voz del ojo / que llamamos pedo, / ruiseñor de los putos*" ("The voice of an eye / we call a fart, / nightingale of fags")[23] and discusses the entertainment value of juxtaposing human faces and buttocks together with their expressive orifices in a picaresque context.

A sense of "modernity" (the awareness of new situations, new relationships, new paradoxes) pervades *El arco y la lira*. The desire expressed in that essay for a far-reaching "incarnation" of poetry in the life of the world is the modernist equivalent of Miguel de Unamuno's romantic desire for immortality as expressed in *Del sentimiento trágico de la vida*. Poetry and society form another duality. Paz

writes in the epilogue ("Los signos en rotación") to *El arco y la lira*
that although society is never poetic by nature "a society without
poetry would lack language: everyone would be saying the same
thing, or nobody would be speaking." (253–54) Although poetic incarnation in a meaningful form of social reality is as impossible as
the incarnation Unamuno sought in immortality, society needs it
and in countless ways strives for it.

The world, of course, imposes itself on the whole spectrum of arts
and letters. Recognizing its intrusion is a vital part of what Paz, Harold Rosenberg, and others have called the modern tradition or tradition of the new (again, dichotomy prevails), because contrast or
intentional juxtaposition bears the seeds of disruption. As a theorist
Paz seems to base his idea of modernity on a sequence of dichotomy
and dispersal: dichotomy understood as existential ruptures or contradictions like those I've referred to. The concept of dichotomy implies that the creative process and critical consciousness—admirably
balanced in Paz's writing—are reciprocal, and that the word "tradition" in the modern era is definable only in light of the excisions
and changes that transfigure it. Dispersal, in turn, is attributed to
the inevitable fragmentation of a world that according to most reli-
gions and myths was in the remote past harmonious and unified.
The image of Spain as "*madre patria*" (*mother-father:* still another dichotomy) of Hispanic America is one aspect of that unifying concept. Every historian of Hispanic-American literature is aware of that
persistent parental survival. Yet the Hispanic-American *patrias* or
son-daughter nations of the Western Hemisphere go their own way;
their cultures grow, advance, detour, transform themselves, and re-
trace their steps. Artists and writers acquire a double consciousness
in which the lost past merges with a present in dispersal.

In the light of those two concepts—dichotomy, dispersal—the circumstances of Hispanic-American poetry over the centuries become
more comprehensible. "When did we begin to sense that we were
different," asks Paz in "Alrededores de la literature hispanoamericana," and observes that Sor Juana Inés de la Cruz (1651–95) was
the first important poet to reveal an awareness of her double (His-
pano-Mexican) identity.[24] Here and in other essays he echoes the
peripheral view that Ortega y Gasset had previously applied to Spain.
Ortega thought of his compatriots "totally and purely European,
precisely the most extreme variety of European, very close to the
'completely other.' "[25] Years later and with or without Ortega's state-

ment in mind, Paz disdainfully extends the extremist idea to Hispanic Americans, himself included, calling them an extreme of Western culture—"an eccentric, deficient and dissonant extreme."[26]

In the first edition of *El laberinto de la soledad* (1950) he defines the Mexican situation as a search for historical identity through a ceaseless struggle between the love of form and the love of spontaneity. In *El laberinto* of 1950 he reveals intuitions of his emphasis in a variety of later works on "the other," referring to Mexicans as historical and spiritual "orphans." But at the same time he asserts that Mexican literature is a new and vigorous element of universal culture and, further, part of an extensive Hispanic-American enrichment of Spanish culture. In a positive sense Paz is saying that Hispanic culture is in a state of continuous intellectual expansion. In a negative sense—beginning in 1956 with the first edition of *El arco y la lira*—he believes that the future is vanishing as a factor in twentieth-century thought. And in the epilogue ("Los signos en rotación") to the second edition (1967) he darkly reaffirms that view: "Our time is the end of history as an imaginable or foreseeable future," because time, in the abstract desert of technology, is discontinuous and loses us.[27]

"Otherness" becomes an exterior, maybe an estrangement. Technology blurs traditional concepts of space and time.[28] The center seems to be nowhere; chaos may absorb the landscape. While at Harvard as Charles Eliot Norton Professor of Poetry, Paz wrote what could be considered his appendix to the concept of a vanishing future just quoted. It appears as an apocalypse *sottovoce* in "Paisaje immemorial." The poem—one of his finest—is dated February 23, 1972, and I've often wondered if it was snowing in Cambridge the day or the night he wrote it. These are its concluding lines:

> *Un día*   ("One day
> *en los tallos de hierro*   on their stems of iron
> *estallarán las lámparas*   streetlights will explode
> *Un día*   One day
> *el mugido de los motores*   the lowing of motors
> *ha de apagarse*   will cease
> *Un día*   One day
> *estas casas serán colinas*   these houses will be hills
> *otra vez*   again
> *hablarel viento entre las piedras*   wind through the rocks

hablará a solas	will speak unheard
Oblicua	Obliquely
entre las sombras	among shadows
insombra	transparently
ha de caer	it will fall
casi azul	almost blue
sobre la tierra	over the earth
La misma de ahora	The same as now
la nieve de hace un millón de años	the snow of a million years ago")

The poem, with its "snow of a million years ago," has absorbed history and time; it's part of the author's trend toward a fusion of the material and the immaterial in most of his lyrics since the 1970s, notably *El mono gramático* (1974), *Vuelta* (1976), and *Arbol adentro* (1987).[29]

The future, which Paz has seen as metaphorically diminished, still forces its meaning upon us: it's still an enigma we must question and try to decipher—just as the past—with its Reciprocal Discovery of 1492, its fallen angels and its unrecorded sunsets—is also an enigma. For the same reason, memory is creative. Past writing or experiences recalled from one's youth are still an element of one's maturity. And whether the author intends it or not, those writings or recollections surpass any later contradiction between a negative or celebratory sense of the world. In "Poesía e historia," (1983) Paz speaks of the unifying quality of poetry in the most turbulent times, and his testimony is an appropriate conclusion to this chapter:

> In Mexico those of us who were twenty-five years old in 1940 mentally set the figures of our poets against those of the tyrants: Darío, Machado and Juan Ramón shielded us from the Francos, Somozas and Trujillos. But for us poetry was neither a refuge nor an escape: it was an awareness and a fidelity. It united that which history had divided. In the face of ruin and disintegrated projects we watched the erection of diaphanous structures. Poetry was continuity.[30]

4

On Picaresque Progress

Determiné de pasarme a Indias . . .
y fueme peor.
—Francisco de Quevedo, *Historia de la vida del Buscón*

PROBABLY IN DEFERENCE TO THE SPANISH GOLDEN AGE, PICARESQUE
literature is largely relegated to its canonical past. Attention still cen-
ters on sixteenth- and seventeenth-century models of a resilient
rogue who undergoes a short evolution that begins with an anonymous work, *La vida de Lazarillo de Tormes* (1554), flowers with Mateo
Alemán's *Guzmán de Alfarache* (1599 and 1604), and culminates in
Francisco Quevedo's *Historia de la Vida del Buscón* (1626). Due partly
to the influence of that triumvirate of figures, an image of the pícaro
as noticeably local and dated has endured.

But many readers—this one included—think the pícaro deserves
a broader literary status, one that transcends its type or stereotype.
We believe the figure in its antiheroic manifestations is more important as the performance of an *attitude* than as a generic *character*. European and North and South American writers of every era have
long shared the picaresque mode, which is also utilized by a variety
of other performers. Consider these examples:

Charlie Chaplin (exemplary man-child of the twentieth century),
when cornered by an oversized but slow-witted bully, a policeman
on his beat, or an irate restaurant manager seeking payment of his
check, respectfully tips his hat a split-second before he dodges and
tries to escape.

Casey Stengel at bat—referred to in chapter 1—gracefully "gives
the bird" to a stadium full of Dodger fans.

In October 1996 the Philadelphia Orchestra is on strike. Independently of their management, the musicians organize a few concerts
to make up some of their losses in salary and benefits. A subtle sym-

bol of their problem is the inclusion on a program conducted in Media, Pennsylvania by Luis Biava of Josef Haydn's "Farewell Symphony," no. 45 (1792). In the last movement of that work the orchestra disappears one by one until only four first-chair string players remain on stage. Then there are three, two, and—finally— just one (the concert master) who plays the last notes and leaves the stage alone. Thus performed, the composition is in the picaresque mode of Haydn, whose own motive in writing it had been his patron's unwillingness to grant his musicians Christmas-vacation time. The musicians of 1996 were saying in an equally lighthearted way that the Philadelphia management had not negotiated in good faith.

Furthermore, picaresque action can be simply capricious, such as adding a black moustache to Leonardo da Vinci's "Mona Lisa," or overtly antiintellectual, like the Perón administration's appointment in 1946 of Jorge Luis Borges as Chief Chicken Inspector for Buenos Aires. Or think of Andy Warhol's method as seen by David Bosworth: "In a society ruled by salesmanship . . . the key was not *what you made*, so much as *where you placed it*. . . . All he had to do, Warhol deduced, was to supply a reflecting pond, and if he hung it on the right wall, every Narcissus passing by would be bound to find it beautiful."[1] Like the King and the Duke with their traveling theater in *Huckleberry Finn* and Chaplin tipping his hat, Warhol the Mimic was primarily interested in what he could get away with.

Finally, a more emphatic instance of the rogue's caprice at work was the dynamiting (ca. 1978) by a young sculptor in Milan of the gallery in which his own works were on exhibit. In the spirit of the best rogues, composition was inseparable from performance; the resourceful sculptor offered a display of stable forms in pulverized motion. To blow up one's creation is the ultimate form of artistic expression, he thought—albeit at the probable cost of oblivion. (*Ars longa, vita brevis?* Or is it vice versa?) I, for one, have forgotten the sculptor's name, and his explosion in Milan is unlikely to figure prominently in future histories of art.

Happily, several scholars in the twentieth century have ventured beyond the pigeonholing approach that limited the mode to a narrow Spanish tradition. In a pioneering essay first published in 1962 ("Toward a Definition of the Picaresque") Claudio Guillén suggests that the tradition has survived in mythical ways.[2] In a lucid 1974 article Ulrich Wicks advocates a "modal approach," and the survival theory, with its inevitable bifurcations, has found strong support in books by Robert Alter, *Rogue's Progress* (1964), and Alexander Blackburn, *The Myth of the Pícaro* (1979).[3] These studies have led to a perception of the picaresque sense of life as a literary and historical expansion, and that is what is now being discussed in a quite broad cultural context.

As a form, picaresque story telling is not of major importance. Its power resides in its *functions*, which in many different ways express an attitude based on calculation and guile. In general, a closer examination of how the picaresque attitude has extended itself (in both time and space) is needed. An old proverb, also a botanical metaphor, could be helpful: "*La mala yerba nunca muere.*" Like most unwanted flora that creep into our gardens, the picaresque spirit endures, and important manifestations of it on both sides of the Atlantic have been duly recognized. Starting in the eighteenth century, they include Defoe's *Moll Flanders* and Fielding's *Tom Jones* in England; Cela's *La familia de Pascual Duarte* and Suárez Carreño's *Las últimas horas* in Spain; Fernández de Lizardi's *El Periquillo Sarniento* and Romero's *La vida inútil de Pito Pérez* in Mexico; Hernández's *Martín Fierro* and parts of Marechal's *Adán Buenosayres* in Argentina; Mark Twain's *Huckleberry Finn* and Bellow's *The Adventures of Augie March* in the United States; Rojas's *Hijo de Ladrón* and Allende's *Eva Luna* in Chile. Notice that the titles of all but one of these works specifically identify an outcast or alienated protagonist. As such, the protagonist embodies a problematical social existence and cultural point of view rather than the inner or outer complexities of a particular person.

But these same neo- or post- or semi-picaresque examples have been read largely as part of a deteriorating genre. That's understandable at least in one sense, because—even during its prime in the sixteenth and seventeenth centuries—the picaresque novel itself was an explicit deterioration of something else: the intentional degradation of chivalric or heroic models. Still, the garden weed refuses to die, which is why Harry Sieber's observation that Smollett's *The Adventures of Roderick Random* (1748) was an "already disintegrated picaresque novel" amounts to a distortion.[4] Actually the pícaro creature—a species up-from-under and only partly controlled by its formal authors—has adapted itself by trial, trickery and error to the modern world's chaotic circumstances. It's a species that includes the type, in Guillén's apt phrase, of "coward with a cause," but which is also a virus of the spirit, a contagious force that affects and infects many other persons ranging from cowards to allegedly solid citizens.[5]

One purpose of this essay is to discover the pervasive force that moves not only the central actor by the title of the work in which he or she appears—as in those mentioned above—but also other characters that he or she encounters and, especially, the author's own view of things. Equally important are the various means of survival or semi-survival by which the picaresque organism, this enduring yet susceptible human weed, keeps growing. The pervasive force, first, affects the first-person narrator who adapts in a parasitic or subliminal way to the conditions of his or her environment. In the second place and contradictorily, the participating narrator's unguarded state becomes educational, experienced as it is in adverse and unforgettable ways. Thus, the pícaro enjoys a certain authorial consciousness and shows critical insights comparable to those found in the best works of fiction of any kind. The genre's broad scope for future writing is symbolically present in the opulent title of a seventeenth-century edition of Quevedo's novel: *Historia de la vida del Buscón llamado don Pablos, ejemplo de vagamundos y espejo de tacaños.*

But probably the pícaro's biggest asset is an aptitude (with the assisting author's sensitive collaboration, of course) for self-invention, which is also a means of self-protection and—at meaningful moments—revenge. He or she is not so much the antihero as a nimble performer: a warped mirror, as Ramón del Valle Inclán would have it, of the world's conflictive interests over the past five hundred years. In that shifting instrumental role the pícaro maneuvers and gesticulates against the limits of social conformity, but for lack of resources and true determination, falls short of revolution. In Pérez Galdós's *Fortunata y Jacinta,* the religiously inspired philanthropist Guillermina Pacheco is determined to educate and reform a rough character named Mauricia la Dura. In her illuminating study of the novel Harriet Turner has pointed (in a nineteenth-century context) to what could be called a surreptitious pact with charity. As Turner reminds us, Mauricia's raucous behavior and prostitute's view of life need not obscure the saintly Guillermina's willingness to pickpocket affluent gentlemen to assure that they help finance her orphanage.[6]

The picaresque spirit characteristically works within limits, but the dimensions of its outreach are virtually unlimited. As I've suggested with examples of the Philadelphia Orchestra on strike, Charlie Chaplin's sleight-of-hand and foot, the dynamitic sculptor in Milan, tomato-soup mimesis, and the appointment of Jorge Luis Borges as chicken inspector for Buenos Aires, that spirit is literarily important because it underlies, transcends, and is independent of literature. Further, the celebrated or notorious persons of the real world who embody the picaresque enhance themselves in strikingly fictitious ways; self-invention has never been the exclusive province of the writer, the artist, the actor, or the madman. It's also what Aristotle ("Ari") Onassis has in common with Artemio Cruz, Howard Hughes with Jay ("The Great") Gatsby; and Eva Perón—the fatherless child who sets forth from Junín to seek her fortune—partly with the self-romanticizing Emma Bovary and partly with Citizen Kane the demagogue—who, in turn, was modeled by Orson Welles on a wheeling-and-dealing publisher, William Randolph Hearst.

With those figures and their dubious functions in mind, we can think of pícaros as both profoundly traditional and vitally up-to-date. They show how the power of appearance is bought at the cost of honest perception. Those who partake of it in today's world know that the great questions submerged in Hamlet's sea of troubles amount to little compared to the applied sciences of advertising and one-upmanship. The most resourceful sharpies of the twentieth and the current centuries form flexible think tanks that include entrepreneurs, insiders, p.r. consultants, lobby groups, photo-op politicians, TV evangelists, assorted criminals, and the chorus of used-car salesmen in chapter 7 of John Steinbeck's *The Grapes of Wrath*. All these promoters have given Boobus Americanus what appeals in a picaresque way to his vindictive ego: Bart Simpson in and out of elementary school, Dennis Rodman on and off the basketball court, Tammy Bakker's televised tears, Rush Limbaugh's radio mouth.

Performance is what counts, as Onassis the shipping magnate sensed when, many years after the alleged and unsubstantiated fact, he claimed to have slept with Eva Perón during her stay at the Hotel de Paris in Monte Carlo in 1947.[7] Undoubtedly Onassis was also aware of the venerable art of gossip as a generative force for spreading the picaresque appeal to innumerable listeners and potential communicators. *Las malas lenguas:* gossip lends itself naturally to the storyteller's imagination; it resonates in the mind's ear. Well before García Márquez completed his Remedios-la-bella episode of the rising sheets, enabling the beauty queen of *Cien años de soledad* to as-

cend on a windy March afternoon to her realm of oblivion, several
amateur narrators had helped him with his research on the "real"
exile from a small Colombian town of a pregnant but unmarried
young woman (as explained by her socially correct mother, the
young woman had simply died and taken her appropriate place in
heaven). It was up to the author to transform the event into the levi-
tating miracle of his novel.[8]

Paradoxically, the pícaro's problematical social existence and
alienated cultural view of the world lend themselves to the figure's
diversity of expression and methods of dynamic self-creation. The
pícaro's modern progress entails a process that has contributed to
portrayals as different as the basically benevolent Charlie Chaplin
and Carlos Fuentes's ultraresourceful macho man, Artemio Cruz.
One rogue as underdog, another as top dog, so to speak. As the latter, the multimillionaire Congressman Cruz, puts it: "We're men,
not martyrs: anything goes as long as we're in control; whoever loses
control is screwed."[9] Lose control and you're done for. The cantankerous blind man in *Lazarillo de Tormes* (Tratado Primero) had already discovered that when, following his young guide's malicious
instructions, he jumped as hard as he could against a stone pillar.

Like any other creature, the pícaro undergoes an endless evolution, a series of adaptive changes that vary according to time and
place. Historically, the process confirms Darwin's theory of natural
selection. One thinks of a forest or jungle in which nature's species
(like literary genres, or what Alfonso Reyes more suggestively calls
"functions") thrive, mutate, grow stronger or weaker, or simply die
out.

In what follows the spreading-weed species is considered in its
geographical and historical transformations, mainly in Hispanic
America. I believe the Hispanic rogue neither declines nor deterio-
rates with its emigrations after *Historia del Buscón*. Rather, Quevedo's
work—Pablos his protagonist confirms it (*"Determiné de pasarme a Indias . . . y fueme peor"*)—offers itself as a point of departure for the
pícaro's survival and dissemination. Little does it matter that the author failed to produce his promised sequel; the Buscón of our collective imagination did get to the New World and we're free to
speculate on the ways things went worse for him. His transplantation
was his loss and the reader's gain.

The dissemination manifests itself in some unexpected places and
persons. For example, the basically timid poet Rubén Darío, his

womanizing and lively tributes to Bacchus notwithstanding, has seldom been thought of as a pícaro. Yet, as we read in his *Autobiografía*, the author and self-declared victim of "female felinity" demonstrates how the lyric vocation, a few stiff drinks, and a rogue's tactics can work—albeit precariously—together. In 1912 as he composes his slim memoir, Darío offers a brief, quite hazy recollection of an engagement party many years before in Chinandega, a small provincial capital northwest of León, Nicaragua.

As Darío tells it, he had been turned down by the fiancée, whom he still adored, in favor of a more mature and affluent suitor. Nevertheless, the poet was among the invited guests and—already under the influence of several drinks when he arrived—was asked to recite something appropriate for the occasion. The resourceful versifier was more than willing to comply, launching a vigorous defamation of the *novio*'s character and the *novia*'s entire family. Not surprisingly, before he could finish his performance he was hustled out of the house, and (with quick diplomatic assistance) exiled to El Salvador the next morning.[10]

Very different and still more curious is the account given in Charles D. Watland's biography. There we read that the poet was not acting on his own behalf, but on that of a friend, Francisco Castro, the real former suitor who still loved the fiancée, Narcisa Mayorga. In this version Darío—uninvited but plied with the same "*excitantes del Diablo*"—was to carry out a plot to "rescue" Narcisa, persuading her to escape with him and carrying her off on horseback to join Castro in some secret place. But the poet's preceding drinks and the partiers' unexpected request led to the same immediate result: Rubén began declaiming, and was abruptly escorted out. In this version, however, the exile to El Salvador was not the next morning, because Darío didn't have the money to pay his hotel bill in Chinandega, but some days later, when his generous friend Francisco Castro paid it for him and—for good measure—the penniless poet's ticket to the neighboring country.[11]

One wonders if José Rubén Romero had read or at least heard about that poetic misadventure before completing his Mexican masterpiece, *La vida inútil de Pito Pérez* (1938). Romero's threadbare hero, you'll recall—shared Darío's romantic sentiments and—in a noticeably cruder context—his poetic compulsions, not to forget his bibulous bent. The wedding banquet scenes in the autobiography and the novel are close to identical: Pito appears, uninvited, at the

reception of a former fiancée who has rejected him; and his unwel-
come toast to the groom includes the following tribute to the bride:

> "El pueblo lo felicita
> por la mujer que se lleva.
> Es dadivosa, bonita,
> diligente, y casi nueva."[12]

> [Our village is delighted
> that this woman is for you.
> She's generous, pretty,
> diligent, and almost new.]

The groom, understandably, is not pleased and ends the incident by
accurately slinging a wine bottle at the impromptu bard's head. In
his extra-brief (thirteen page) "Breve historia de mis libros" (1942)
Romero assures us that Pito Pérez really existed. Further, he emphasizes the author's inseparability from his protagonist and literary
partner. "Pito Pérez se ha servido de mí, yo he abusado de Pito
Pérez," [Pito Pérez has accepted my help and I've taken advantage
of Pito Pérez] he confesses.[13] Romero's words reveal, one could say,
one of the methods by which legendary heroes are made.

Alejo Carpentier has said that he wrote his celebrated novel *El recurso del método* (1974) as "la picaresca del dictador," sensing that
in the New World the pícaro "had been magnified in a magnified
continent."[14] Carpentier's theory of magnification and my concept
of diffusion could be considered not as contradictory but complementary. Clearly, the Primer Magistrado of *El recurso del método*, the
superannuated patriarch of García Márquez's *El otoño del Patriarca*
(1975), and General Pitecántropo, another dictator, oversexed and
sporadically mutated into a banana gobbling gorilla), in Demetrio
Aguilera Malta's *El secuestro del general* (1973) are not traditional pica-
roons, but like the latter they inhabit a world moved mainly by self-
interest, deception, and betrayal, and circulate in a society activated
by dandies, other military officers, bureaucrats, ranch owners,
thieves, mistresses, clerics, and diplomats.

In Carpentier's novel one recalls the temporarily exiled Primer
Magistrado's ambassador to France, el Cholo Mendoza, "in his yel-
low gloves, a gardenia in his lapel and light gray spats—as always—
even in the heat of summer," the dictator's daughter Ofelia's
impregnation in Salzburg by a sneaky performer of Papageno's role

in *The Magic Flute,* and a cartoonist of the picaresque paper *Simplicissimus,* in Munich who had portrayed the proud, Europeanized caudillo in a broad-brimmed Mexican hat, crossed cartridge belts and a monumental millionaire's paunch in the act of shooting a poor peasant woman on her knees.[15] Long after his return to power in Nueva Córdoba the learned dictator circumvents Article Thirty-nine of the Constitution of 1910 and maintains himself in office beyond the prescribed six-year term by opportunely remembering that his government has not yet signed a peace treaty with Hungary at the end of World War I. Further, he cynically anticipates that the Hungarian ambassador to Nueva Córdoba, who hasn't been paid for months and has had to resort to pawning his wife's clothes, will lose his diplomatic status and end up playing the violin in a third-rate gypsy tavern. And we should not forget the Magistrado's executive secretary Dr. Peralta who, whenever undesirable, subversive periodicals or books appear in stores of the capital, is promptly dispatched to buy them up and destroy them—spending in that prudent exercise of authority a substantial portion of the federal revenues.

Like several other late twentieth-century Hispanic-American works, including Mario Vargas Llosa's *Pantaleón y las visitadoras,* Tomás Eloy Martínez's *Santa Evita,* García Márquez's *La increíble y triste historia de la cándida Eréndira y de su abuela desalmada* and Luis Rafael Sánchez's *La guaracha del Macho Camacho, El recurso del método* demonstrates how a wide variety of characters can participate simultaneously in the picaresque process.

The justly famous García Márquez shares with Carpentier an addiction to baroque complexity as the appropriate ambience for knavery and corruption. His Patriarch is an even more extravagant creation than the Primer Magistrado. El Patriarca is a colossus of feel-goodism and a permanent spectacle of depravity. He has engendered about five thousand unwanted offspring; his mysteriously perforated scrotum whistles like Scottish bagpipes as he walks; he has reached an age estimated at between 107 and 232 years; and—when his time has come—he graciously sneezes himself to death. The Patriarch, one might say if Carpentier's magnification theory is valid, is the pícaro swollen beyond recognition. His title (*General del Universo*) befits his power and impunity. His accomplishments range from the secret drowning of two thousand children (who are potential witnesses) previously employed in rigging the national lottery three times a week, to the literal roasting of his dissident Minister of

Defense, whose carefully marinated corpse is served at midnight in full military attire on a moist bed of cauliflower, herbs, and laurel leaves to his guests, the perplexed palace guard corps.

García Márquez underscores an important background coincidence between his opulent protagonist and the classic picaroon: that is, each is his mother's son alone. In the Patriarch's case, "everyone knew he was an orphan, like the most illustrious despots in history."[16] As if to increase the significance of that orphanhood, the Patriarch's earthy proletarian mother, Bendición Alvarado, appears in the nation's schoolbooks as having realized an immaculate conception of her celebrated son, and when the Nueva Córdoba government's petition for her canonization in Rome is denied, the papal ambassador's residence is attacked by rock-throwing devotees and churches are burned throughout the capital. The author's hyperbolic vision extends to other characters and situations in his novel, including his magic tale of the U.S. ambassador who in an unspecified year and with full authorization by his government, arranged to have the Caribbean Sea removed in carefully numbered sections from its hurricane environs and relocated in sunny Arizona. Nor should we forget, in García Márquez's novelette *La increíble y triste historia de la cándida Eréndira,* the sweet fourteen-year-old who through the initiative of her enterprising grandmother became the most heavily exploited prostitute in world literature.

It's in the air; it's everywhere. Under no one's particular control, the picaresque spirit has infiltrated a borderless territory of modern life, and the fictional and the real complement each other in the process. Thus, Eva Perón is still with us, and Tomás Eloy Martínez in *Santa Evita* (1993) and Abel Posse in *La passion según Eva* (1994) have revived her hectic rite of passage from underprivileged child to the many-sided and continually disputed legend of today. Thus, W. C. Fields, Cantínflas, and Charlie Chaplin have a living presence on videotape. Thus Irma Serrano's most memorable musical performance, a serenade with mariachis in which she publicly insulted a Mexican president of the 1960s outside his residence at Los Pinos for having jilted her after a five-year intimate relationship, is saucily described in her memoir written in collaboration with Elisa Robledo, *A calzón amarrado* (1978). Thus, in Sinclair Lewis's *Elmer Gantry* (1927) the up-and-coming preacher and one of literature's major hypocrites receives an anonymous donation of thirty dimes wrapped in a religious tract and spends them on pictures of burlesque queens. Thus, in Isabel Allende's *Eva Luna* (1987), the protagonist, taking leave of the most pompous and cantankerous of her employers, removes the chamber pot from under the armchair where he reads, writes, snoozes, and defecates, and ceremoniously empties its contents on his head. Thus, *Picardía mexicana* (first edition, 1960) and *Nueva picardía* (first edition, 1971) by A. Jiménez, bubbling with anecdotes, puns, proverbs, and other improprieties, are perennially reprinted and sold.

Those works, among many others, are part of the evidence that confirms the strength of Pablos el Buscón's legacy. He bequeathed it to the New World and writers of the New World have known how to use it. If the picaresque novel in the strict, limited sense has deteriorated, its mythical power and the spirit that generates it are as vital as ever. It can reasonably be argued that the magical elements in García Márquez' *Cien años de soledad* and *El otoño del patrarca* extend and intensify the picaresque mode. That is, the Colombian writer takes what for the author of *El lazarillo de Tormes* was a traditional kind of retaliation of servant versus employer, or for Mark Twain a comparatively simple exposition of trickery in the King-and-Duke episodes in *Huckleberry Finn* and converts them into his own kind of ironical magic.

Accordingly, near the beginning of *Cien años de soledad* an amber-colored syrup concocted by gypsies and guaranteed to make whoever takes it invisible is swallowed by the "taciturn Armenian" who peddles it and as a result is reduced to a quickly evaporating puddle. Here, as well as in the Remedios-la-bella episode commented on earlier in this chapter, the novelist demonstrates that for him reality is fertile raw material for situations that are potentially poetic, ironic, or picaresque.

In every work discussed in this chapter the basic pîcaro—the true manipulator—is the author him- or herself. The picaresque essence, including whatever Pablos el Buscón, Pito Pérez, Remedios la bella, or Eva Luna seem to represent, is in the eye of the resourceful—and ironic—beholder. It feeds on the self-protecting instincts, gossip, and other forms of creative revision that only such a beholder can bring to light. We should recognize, in conclusion, that the process of devaluation so often attributed to the skepticism of fashionable postmodernists has *always* been operative in narrative writing—especially in its picaresque manifestations.

Loren Eisley, the distinguished naturalist and one of the

twentieth-century's finest essayists, wrote that the human being is really "a cosmic orphan" who never finds a home, a subject "of uncertain beginnings and an indefinite ending."[17] The pícaro may well be an existentially intensified version of that orphan, a human being who stimulates the artist as a compassionate skeptic (or the compassionate skeptic as artist). Further, we can assume that the uncertainty and indefiniteness referred to by Eisley are not in a literary sense any kind of barrier or burden. Rather, they can be be accepted as the unsettled condition of the pícaro's solitude, and continuous passage through the magical landscape of the writer's imagination.

5

Ortega y Gasset in Argentina:
The Exasperating Colony

¿Qué va a hacer en Corrientes un
fantasma como yo?

             —J.O. y G.

IN A QUESTION-AND-ANSWER SESSION FOLLOWING HIS PUBLIC LECTURE
at the University of Pennsylvania on April 15, 1983, Jorge Luis
Borges was asked what he thought of José Ortega y Gasset. To the
amusement of some and surprise of others in the large audience,
Borges casually replied, "I met him only once; a rather boring gentleman, I must say." Then, as if to soften a judgment he quickly
sensed was careless, he conceded that the boredom may well have
been reciprocal.

To be sure, the two writers had little in common, and neither one
when they met (probably in 1928) had much to offer the other. Although they shared a consistent interest in the relationship between
philosophy and literature, their educational backgrounds, personalities, and cultural outlooks were basically different. In the 1920s Ortega was viewed in Buenos Aires as the *monstruo sagrado* of a Spanish
intelligentsia whose horizons were largely European; Borges (six-
teen years younger) was a little-known critic (outside Argentina) and
experimentalist in a minor Hispanic-American vanguard. Years
passed, but Borges was not to gain with maturity a reputation for
evenhandedness in his critical evaluations. With or without its hasty
amendment, the spontaneous evaluation of Ortega was intellectually frivolous.

But the off-handed breach of decorum I've referred to is not, in
itself, of major importance. Rather, it is a revealing symptom of cultural incompatibility. It is also a key to the case history of an influen-

75

tial European's commitment to cultural colonialism, in the context of his probable motivation and literary refinements. Ortega's view of Argentina and the New World was noticeably colored by his intellectual narcissism, which was exacerbated—in turn—by his progressive alienation from the Spanish Republic. Well before the 1930s he had tended to base historical and metaphysical conclusions on sense—usually visual—impressions. This idiosyncrasy made much of the world, and especially Hispanic America, strange to him. In exploring his perspectivist inclination I endeavored to combine the most germane historical and biographical factors with the most pertinent literary and philosophical ones. The result has been a generally negative portrait.

Discerning students of literature are aware that intention is but one part of language. Words often reveal something not fully comprehended by the speaker or writer who uses them. Words function as echo chambers, masks, or mirrors; and one suspects that behind them obscure demiurges may be at work. Those demiurges, or spirits, or gods of an unknown hierarchy are among the true voices of literature and, in varying degree, of the critical responses to which literature may lead.

As both Ortega and Borges seem to believe, in literature and art, *mentalities* are necessarily *perspectives*. The incompatibility revealed in Borges's spontaneous recollection of Ortega was between two perspectives: the Hispano-European and the Hispano-American. In the 1920s and 1930s when Ortega was a figure of high literary fashion, Argentine, Peruvian, and Mexican intellectuals demanded innovation from the Hispanic-American writer. From the European writer they sought instructiveness. The implied comparison was an unequal one. The New World, for most Europeans, was still a geographical garden in which the Old World's seeds of thought might be cultivated. Certainly there was much in Ortega's philosophy of "vital reason" that appealed to his American readers and even to American readers unfamiliar with his works. The concept of being as reason versus the concept of being as experience (and vice versa) was a conflict which—precisely because it defied solution—was the nucleus of Ortega's circumstantial thought. It could also be considered an inevitable issue for Hispanic America's circumstantial culture.

Between his first visit to Argentina in 1916 and his final departure in 1942 Ortega y Gasset became a legend; and posthumously, in

1956, the Argentine philosopher Francisco Romero would dub him *jefe espiritual*, no less, of the Hispanic world.[1] In Romero's view, Ortega has fulfilled a function comparable to those of Menéndez y Pelayo in late nineteenth-century Spain and Croce in early twentieth-century Italy. By contrast Miguel de Unamuno, thought the author of *Teoría del hombre*, had lacked the requisite "objectivity, serenity and universality" to compete for the title. Now, in the penumbra of Ortega's death and the pointed unrecognition of his work by the Franco government and the Spanish religious hierarchy, Romero was comparing him to the Cid, who was destined to win additional battles in the hereafter.

Ortega, of course, has won a few battles of that kind, the most important of which is continuing to be read. *La deshumanización del arte* (1925), *La rebelión de las masas* (1930) and *El tema de nuestro tiempo* (1923) are lucid essays that steer the reader toward constructive re-evaluations. He was not the first to criticize the elevation of mediocrity to a level close to that of excellence, but no one has done it more eloquently than he. Whatever may disturb us about Ortega—a certain haughtiness, a tendency to impose arbitrary limits on the world's cultures, his political ambiguities, for example—Borges's snap characterization deserves rejection; Ortega is hardly ever boring. Many of his representative pieces were written for a listening audience, and he spoke with the finest intuitions of Narcissus. His thought has a musical symmetry. In contrast to Unamuno, he kept a prudent distance from the situations he analyzed. He was the clairvoyant European during Europe's most turbulent and confusing period. In *La rebelión de las masas* he declared a truth later repeated by others in several ways: violence in the modern world is more often considered as an expected practice than as a primitive aberration.

Nevertheless, there was something basically incompatible in Ortega with both the New World spirit and New World realities. He did not seem to sense the former nor to perceive the latter. There's little doubt that Eduardo Mallea had him in mind when he wrote in *Historia de una pasión argentina* (1937):

> I conversed, I met some intellectuals from abroad. They were extremely intelligent men who came to our country to tell us beautiful things; but when they left they knew our way of life no better than when they arrived. Philosophers, thinkers, writers who persisted—due to an inevitable weakness of intellect—in accommodating our moral land-

scape to the dialectical biases they came here with; they were born professors; brilliant on the podium; yet downright trivial in their human comprehension![2]

During his three visits to Argentina (1916, 1928, 1939 to 1942) Ortega's problem appears to have been twofold: shortsightedness in his evaluations, and an inability or unwillingness to communicate with Argentines on a mutually acceptable level.

The lack of vision—or his distorted vision—was due in part to the dialectical biases referred to by Mallea, the perspectivist system by which he had organized his cultural concepts, and in part to his facile acceptance of G.W. F. Hegel's view of the Americas in the latter's *Philosophy of History*, which led the Spanish thinker almost to exclude them from the twentieth-century world community. Steadfast in his Eurocentric point of view, Hegel had assimilated and enthusiastically synthesized Jean Louis Leclerc Buffon's and Cornelius De Pauw's pseudo-scientific explanations of the "inferior" zoological and human species in the New World. "America has always shown itself and continues to show itself as physically and spiritually impotent," he declared in his famous work.[3] Worthy of mention is the fact that Ortega's essay "Hegel y América" was written in 1928, the same year that his *Revista de Occidente*'s publishing division produced the *Philosophy of History* in Spanish translation.

The Spaniard's essay has numerous and extensive quotations from the German's pronouncements on America's alleged immaturity, its weak and undersized fauna, and its prolonged prehistoric stagnation in Nature. Ortega insinuates in this spirited homage to the father of modern logic that he too, a full century later, is waiting for America, with its full endowment of "nueva y saludable barbarie," to shove its way into the mainstream of history. But so far, primitive space had not given way to civilized time: "Where space abounds, nature takes possession of man. Space is a geographical entity, not a historical one."[4] That is not really a functioning idea, but a tautology that Ortega raises to the level of an obsession, and which five years later Ezequiel Martínez Estrada incorporates—with quite different motivation—into the spatial imagery of *Radiografía de la pampa* (1933).

Whereas Martínez Estrada's book develops a theory of Argentine history (applicable to Hispanic-American history in general) based on the transformation of sixteenth-century Spanish adventurism into progressive American disillusionment, Ortega's short essays on South America—a tiny portion of his extensive complete work, are more in the category of a lately arrived traveler's impressions.[5] Few of them deal directly with the realities of New World culture. Martínez Estrada's view of modern Argentina expressed in "Los valores" (the last chapter of *Radiografía de la pampa*), "where everything is yet to be accomplished," is actually close to Ortega's skeptical futurism in "La pampa . . . promesas."[6] But Martínez Estrada had the longer historical vision—taking the past into account as well as the present; and he offered keen insights on Argentine archetypes (Facundo, Rosas, Martín Fierro) that Ortega never concerned himself with. Ortega always gave priority to his own aesthetic experience. Accordingly, he reduced concrete geography to abstract landscapes, specific persons to anonymous figures or groups, and overshadowed present realities with future possibilities. His outward vision was often obstructed by his inward one. One can easily detect confessional overtones in the following observations in "El hombre a la defensiva":

> The typical Argentine's only vocation is becoming the person he imagines himself to be.

> Indeed, the Argentine always sees himself as reflected in his own imagination: Narcissus in the extreme. He's both Narcissus and Narcissus's reflecting pool. He carries it all with him: his reality, his image, his mirror.

> I fully recognize that Narcissism is an element of every sublime soul. But the Argentine is excessively Narcissus, to a radical degree. He absorbs himself in the contemplation of his own image. (*MPJ*, 140–41)

In the first of the ten themes that make up *El tema de nuestro tiempo* (1923) Ortega defined history as the active effects of "the most energetic men" on the masses; but that definition did not turn out to be relevant in his own view of Argentina and Latin America. In a positive sense, in the context of that Spanish intellectual's possible influence, we could look to Martínez Estrada—who used a concept of the Energetic Man to elucidate a national culture. Although Martínez Estrada was not an admirer of Ortega and didn't include him in his broad but disorganized *Panorama de las literaturas* (1946)—a work in which recognition is given to dozens of lesser figures—he did know the Spaniard's work and shared some of his ideas, the Nietz-schian view of the energetic man among them.[7]

When before or during a train trip from Buenos Aires to Mendoza in 1928 Ortega started to think out "La pampa . . . promesas," he seemed to be executing a plan more than an experiment, a plan in which he might have speculated: "Let the Pampa be a symbol of nothing, and I'll write an essay on the consequences of that symbol." He tells us that when one travels through the hills and valleys of Asturias or the cultivated flatlands of central France, one has a sense of proportion; every true landscape has a foreground as well as a background. But this generalization doesn't apply to the Pampa, which is little more than a geometry or abstraction at the writer's disposal. It lacks distinguishing features. The foreground is the same as the background. For Ortega it was a poetic opportunity—as it was for Domingo Sarmiento and Martínez Estrada in historically more meaningful terms: notably in their best known works, *Civilización y barbarie: Vida de Juan Facundo Quiroga* (1845) and *Radiografía de la pampa*. But in such subjective passages Ortega was often at his poetic best:

"On the horizon the pampa opens its body and its veins so that all the unreality associated with airy and celestial things is absorbed by a geometric, empty abstraction of the foreground. There the landscape drinks in the sky, intoxicating itself with fantasies; that's why the pampa's horizon weaves like a drunkard; it floats, undulates and flutters like the edges of a flag in the wind; it's not anchored to the earth; it finds no fixed place." (*MPJ*, 109)

This immersion of the thoughtful subject in an abstract landscape is just the beginning. In the next paragraph the writer refers to thickets and groves in the distance that acquire a flexible, indefinable appearance: "a soft substance susceptible to any possible form. . . . *They're the constant, all-inclusive promise.*" ("La pampa . . . promesas," *MPJ*, 109–10, Ortega's emphasis). It was as the celebrated "Spectator," the restless witness, that Ortega wrote most of his observations on Argentina, and it was no accident that many of these impressions evaporated into metaphorical allusions: *pampa, boscajes, promesas*. It's easy to see how in the essays of *El Espectador* the philosopher-poet assumes the additional task of the theorist. That is, an image leads him to an idea. In this case the horizon, pregnant with mirages, becomes a symbol of promise. Then promise, with the author's sly connotation of promissory (Argentina is not the promised but the promissory land), is the concept that leads him smoothly into a sociocultural theory: Argentine thinkers and writers feed on promissory signs, not the hard currency of achievement. The providential damnation, as Ortega senses it, is sweeping. "So I've concluded that the Argentine is dominated by that unidentifiable sensation of an evaporated life" (*MPJ*, 110). At the end of "La pampa . . . promesas" he bluntly states that only on very rare occasions can the discriminating European (presumably one with Ortega's own perceptive acumen) find an Argentine naturally disposed to live life for its own sake rather than for some lesser purpose. Undoubtedly this unflattering view of the Argentine human species was a primary ingredient of the composite creature that Ortega developed throughout the 1920s—el *hombre masa*, the European hopelessly diminished, contemporary man incorrigibly Americanized.

Two basic weaknesses in Ortega's assessment of Argentina and the Argentines seem evident. The first—which I've just referred to—was his intellectual shortsightedness, combined with a distorted reading of geographical symbols. The second, which seems to have been more deliberate, was his failure to communicate effectively with all but a half-dozen or so Argentines. And of these only one was of notable stature: the essayist, editor, and publisher, Victoria Ocampo. In her biography (*Victoria Ocampo: Against the Wind and the Tide*) Doris Meyer shows the vital importance of this relationship—there was mutual inspiration—and pointedly remarks that in both his 1916 and 1928 visits to Argentina Don José "was more impressed with the qualities of Argentine women—judged according to his standards of perfection—than with those of Argentine men."[8] On the same page she recalls that Ortega himself admitted in his 1924 epilogue to Ocampo's *De Francesca a Beatrice* that the only other Argentines he admired until then were four young female friends of Victoria's whom he had met in 1916. Alfonso Reyes confirms this view in his diary notes for December 4, 1928: "Last Friday I visited Victoria Ocampo for lunch at San Isidro. We were alone. She mentioned with disgust Ortega's coquettish mannerisms during his lectures with the ladies who admire him."[9] In a later entry (January 8, 1930) Reyes shows that he shared—at least for then—Ortega's skepticism regarding Argentine literary life: "My impressions of the Argentine literary atmosphere are progressively worse; here the main concern is not literature but the political in-fighting of literary cliques," (ibid., 297). But in contrast to the author of "Pampa . . . promesas,"

Reyes formed lasting literary friendships in Argentina and developed a sympathetic understanding of Argentine culture.

Doris Meyer further recalls that Argentine reaction to Ortega's
criticism of his host country in "la pampa. . . . promesas" and "El
hombre a la defensiva" was strongly resentful; that Ortega was
moved because of that to publish a third essay ("Por qué he escrito
'El hombre a la defensiva'") in *La Nación* (reproduced in *OC* 4:73);
and that in contrast to nearly all her compatriots Victoria declared
Ortega's message to be necessary and that he had had a constructive
intention in writing it.[10]

But the irony is that Ortega, who in an open letter to an aspiring
Argentine writer in 1924 had criticized young Argentines for their
alleged Narcissism, was a complete Narcissus himself. *Yo soy yo y mi
circunstancia* ("I am I and my circumstance combined") is not just
an existential declaration; it's also an indelible, self-reflecting statement. Elsewhere I have noted that the basic perspective of all essayists is similar to Stendhal's view of the novelist's perspective: the
novelist walks along a road and comments on his surroundings as
they are reflected in a mirror he's holding in his hand. In doing
essentially the same thing, I add, the essayist is more inclined to include *himself*—and what he happens to be thinking at the time—in
the reflection.[11] One evening, the author recalls in "La pampa . . .
promesas," he was taking a walk along a street in Buenos Aires that
we could call Stendhalian. The experience stimulates a Narcissistic
joke that ironically symbolizes his difficulty in communicating and
underscores his self-regarding penchant. On that crowded street he
was suddenly reminded of the philosopher Kant by street vendors
who were hawking late editions of two newspapers, "*La Crítica! La
Razón!*" Of course, Ortega and the vendors were using the same
words in totally different contexts. They were referring to the news
of the day, with which Ortega was unconcerned; he was thinking of
The Critique of Pure Reason, which they had probably not heard about.
A very different light is cast on the incident (one clearly unfavorable
to Don José) in Barbara Aponte's informative chapter ("José Ortega
y Gasset") in her book, *Alfonso Reyes and Spain.* Aponte quotes a letter from Reyes to Amado Alonso (December 11, 1932) in which he
writes that Ortega "shamelessly stole from me a joke about the Kant-
ian hour of Buenos Aires (when, as the afternoon falls, they sell *La
Crítica* and *La Razón* in the streets), something that I told him and I
told him that I was going to write it . . . and that he admired very

much."[12] In the same letter he adds that his Spanish contemporary had treated him shabbily in other ways during and after Ortega's 1928 sojourn in Argentina.

"El hombre a la defensiva" (1929) is considerably longer than "La pampa . . . promesas" and is really its continuation. It emphasizes the alleged hermeticism, materialistic greed, lack of will power, and Narcissistic indulgences of the Argentine male. Ortega finds a synthesis of what is worst in the Argentine psyche in the phenomenon of *guaranguismo*:

"The *guarango* is aggressive. . . . He corroborates his imagined superiority over his fellow being by subjecting him to jokes in the worst taste. If he [i.e., the *guarango*] is especially timid he'll resort to anonymity (Buenos Aires is the city of the anonymous)." (*MPJ*, 145)

In a footnote near the end of "El hombre a la defensiva" he announces a possible expansion of the *guarango* theme under the projected title *Meditación de los guarangos*. Martínez Estrada seems to have helped discourage this uncordial endeavor by writing (under a pseudonym) a pointed critique: "El guarnguismo de Ortega y Gasset."[13] But the Argentine essayist, then hard at work on a cultural diagnosis of his own—to be published two years later under the title *Radiografía de la pampa* (1933)—completes his reply with a thrust of irony, suggesting that Ortega could probably have written his proposed Meditation without leaving Madrid, just as "to meditate it's not indispensable to get out of oneself."

In a nostalgic speech before the Institución Cultural Española de Buenos Aires in late 1939, Ortega recalls his first arrival in Argentina in 1916 as a relative stranger. With elaborate modesty he mentions that a week after his first lecture in the Facultad de Filosofía y Letras, he returned to give his second one, and that not only was the auditorium full but an unruly crowd was assaulting the building and smashing its windows, "simply because of their desire to have a philosophy lesson from a young Galician, totally unknown a week before." (*MPJ*, 200) But "totally unknown" he was not; for he had begun to appear in print in *La Prensa* of Buenos Aires in 1911. In the conclusion of his essay "Problemas culturales" on the alleged decadence of French culture and its strong yet negative effect on Spanish and Argentine intellectuals of the early twentieth century, he proposes the thesis he'll later develop but never change, that of Argentina the Immature:

> Argentines who read this, as well as the Spaniard who writes it, have been educated in an atmosphere of French decadence and, accordingly, are prone to the danger of accepting as evident virtues, as normal culture, what is actually vice, abnormality and weakness. *Argentina in its youthful excesses, Spain in its fatigue and decrepitude,* have accepted the claims of literary and intellectual power that France attributes to itself as an ornament of the political power given it as a rightful heritage of its revolution and Napoleonic campaigns. That's exactly why—since we were born and raised in a French environment—we should expose it and react against it, if we recognize the fact that it's useless to us.[14]

In justice to Ortega, the twenty-eight-year-old quite liberal thinker of 1911, it should be remembered that he was then balancing in an evenhanded way the Immature-Argentine thesis with the Decrepit-Spain one. His motivation at the time, which he would develop further in *Meditaciones del Quijote, El tema de nuestro tiempo* and *España invertebrada,* was intellectual heroism and Spain's need for new spiritual orientation. Without formally acknowledging it, he was a natural young brother of the Generation of 1898. His diagnosis of Spain's troubles centered on its inherent *dissociations,* as he points out in a chapter ("El imperio de las masas") of *España invertebrada.* Domingo Sarmiento had said essentially the same thing about Argentina in *Civilización y barbarie: Vida de Juan Facundo Quiroga* (1845). Modern Spain still lacked an "articulated" society comparable to those of England, France, and Germany. And, although he did not deliberately apply his dissociation-thesis to Argentina, there's a noticeable affinity between his growing disillusionment with Spanish culture from 1914 on and his permanently skeptical view of culture afloat the pampas.[15] Ortega's eye, as well as his mind, worked as a symbol-scavenger. In "Historia y geografía" (1922) he expressed the idea that georgraphy is not significant as a determining factor but rather as symptom ("síntoma y símbolo") of a people's character: "Castilla es tan terriblemente árida porque es árido el hombre castellano." (*OC* 2:371–73)

This, of course, is a clear example of Ortega's basic perspectivism which, in turn, appears to reflect an absorbent reading of Schopenhauer's opening statement in *The World as Will and Idea* (1818; 2nd, revised ed., 1844), "The world is my idea," and may also have influenced Martínez Estrada's symbolic view of the pampa. Martínez Estrada's "Trapalanda" (title of the first of six sections comprising

Raduiografía de la pampa) is essentially a place—or vague space—to get lost, and could be called the psychological equivalent of Ortega's promissory pampa. Both are situated in an illusory landscape; both are vainly futuristic and based on a past devoid of conscious history; both express metaphorically the modern intellectual's solitude.

A close comparison between everything Ortega wrote about Argentina and the New World and Martínez Estrada's lugubrious visions would show that the latter held out considerably more hope for future improvement than did the former. The Argentine essayist's basic works from *Radiografía de la pampa* (1933) to *El mundo maravilloso de Guillermo Enrique Hudson* (1951) are a relentless scrutiny but also a catharsis of the nation's historical infirmities; and while he offered little in the way of solutions, he was quite specific in analyzing the Argentine psyche as reflected in its archetypes—literary, political, and social. On the other hand, Ortega as an observer of Hispanic America practiced a peculiar cruelty of the abstract. His vaguely configured "America" was not so much the habitatat of incomprehensible beings as a territory devoid of significance. His interpretation usually had the suggestion of a dismissal *a priori*. He didn't look *at* his Argentine contemporaries; he looked past them, in the manner of one who, on entering a room full of cordial people, is struck by the view from a window on the opposite wall. When he did actually address or refer to Argentines in his writings, it was in the same inevitable pattern: the anonymous plural. His pointed contrasts between an emphatic, vacuous kind of Argentine male and the handful of half-human, half-divine Argentine females of his acquaintance were not just an indirect manifestation of amorous enthusiasm; they were also a clear manifestation of Ortega y Gasset's incorrigible Narcissism stressed earlier in this chapter.[16] His self-centeredness made intellectual communication especially difficult for him. Indisputably, "*Yo soy yo y mi circunstancia*" was a self-reflecting statement that magnified the importance of the subject as related to its objects. That relationship is a fundamental element of Ortega's aristocratic logic: psychologically Narcissistic, intellectually elitist, socially anti-egalitarian. He was always one of the few striving to hold his own against the many. His awareness of that struggle became his reason for being.

Ortega's two principal credos—perspectivism as articulated in *Meditaciones del Quijote* and elitisim as conclusively set forth in *La rebelión de las masas* reached their exacerbated form in his commentaries on Argentina, in the distance he increasingly felt between himself and his Argentine contemporaries. He was the subject, irreconcilably estranged from its debased *object-subjects*, i.e., those culturally disenfranchised Latin Americans whom he relegated to a neocolonial status. Clearly, he had arrived in the colonizing spirit, impelled, as he recalls in an article in *La Nación* (April 6, 1924) by the time-honored motto of aristocrats: "el sublime *Noblesse oblige*" (*MPJ*, 54) in which he saw the true foundation of self-discipline. In the same article he adds that the most important aspect of self-discipline he prescribes for the young generation of Argentines is a proper use of influences. "The young must be open to influence. A hermetic youth that excludes exemplary models of life refuses to develop the hidden treasure of ideas and emotions that are sure to function as magnificent organic stimulations." Martin Stabb has noticed Ortega's probable impact (together with Spengler's) on one young writer of questionable distinction in the 1920s: Miguel Angel Virasoro (1900–1965), who developed a historical philosophy in the "sportive" tradition that Ortega felt was lacking among Argentina's young intellectuals. In two essays "El problema de la cultura y la nueva mentalidad argentina and "Introducción a la nueva sensibilidad" published the short-lived review *Inicial*, 1 (December, 1924), and 2 (August, 1925) Virasoro stressed the need for young nations to recover the vigor, spontaneity, and sportive spirit exemplified by pre-Socratic Greece and later lost under "Latin-Judaic" influences. As Stabb points out, *Inicial* was an organ of the far right, dedicated to combating "international communism and the Judaizing press." He notes that Ortega's readers will find "many ideas similar to those expressed in the Spanish essayist's 'Origen deportivo del estado'— composed, incidentally, in 1924."[17] Virasoro, to be sure, was open to the Spaniard's influence, but it was clearly limited. His Spartan enthusiasm showed more reactionary heat than meditative light, and with it he took an unmistakable detour from Ortega's intended enlightenment.

In his better known "Carta a un joven argentino que estudia filosofía" of that era (circa 1924) Ortega finds too much emphasis and a lack of precision: "You [young Argentines] are more receptive than precise, and as long as that doesn't change you'll be entirely dependent on Europe in intellectual matters." (*MPJ*, 68–69) At this point we might ask ourselves if Ortega himself was too much of the opposite persuasion (more precise than receptive), whether the phi-

losopher's penchant for logical discriminations obstructed the
poet's love of everyday communication with nature, the cosmos,
one's fellow man, whether his theoretic compulsions weakened his
grasp on reality. The more one considers the cultural orientation
of his work after 1930, to which the skepticism of "El hombre a la
defensiva," "Por qué he escrito 'El hombre a la defensiva'" and *La
rebelión de las masas* can be considered as a prelude, the more one
becomes aware of his progressive withdrawal from the contemporary
world. That process lasted little more than a decade, and Argentina—from September 1939 to February 1942—turned out to be his
unhappy haven for the political nadir of his life.

He was unhappy not just because of his personal isolation and sporadic depressions, his mother's death in April 1939, and his frail
physical state (he had been given a 50–50 chance of surviving a gall
bladder operation in Paris in October 1938), but also because his
uneasy aloofness from the Spanish Civil War from its beginning
(and from the great majority of Spanish intellectuals-in-exile after
its end) had severely inhibited his freedom of thought. A young Argentine of his acquaintance in the period from 1939 to 1942 writes:
"Over my long, close relationship with Ortega I never heard him
refer to the prevailing situation in Spain, nor to the civil war, nor to
its opposing forces. Clearly, this was a restriction that Ortega wanted
to impose on himself, one that he scrupulously obeyed."[18] The statement reflects accurately the image Ortega himself wanted to propa-
gate; it also reflects a widespread tendency to forget that Don José's
aloofness was far from impartial or objective.

His pointed silence was the continuation of a withdrawal that had
undergone a steady evolution. His disenchantment with the Spanish
Republic antedated the civil war and became public knowledge on
December 6, 1931 in a speech at the Cine de la Opera in Madrid
("Rectificación de la República"). Then, on October 29 of the following year he and two other founders of "Agrupación al Servicio
de la República" (Gregorio Marañón and Ramón Pérez de Ayala)
declared that the Agrupación no longer existed.[19] As violence in
Spain spread from 1933 on, Ortega's political alienation increased.
The intellectual leader "at the service of the Republic" chose to
abandon the Republic as soon as the going got rough. In justice to
Ortega, it's true that the personal ambitions of many political leaders had seriously undermined their government's constitutional
foundation. But withdrawal followed by sustained silence was

scarcely the recourse expected of him by his more hopeful contemporaries. Still less appropriate was the intensification of his attitude when hostilities broke out in July of 1936. The Spanish Civil War was a time for choosing sides, not only in Spain but throughout the Western World; and no conscientious observer in the Western World could ignore the polarization of allegiances that quickly and permanently set in. Nevertheless, Ortega granted himself a special immunity, which—in the light of some quite unambiguous opinions he expressed during his exile—is hard to justify. His recalcitrance further aggravated his estrangement from the Argentine intelligentsia—Victoria Ocampo excepted—that had been growing on its own since he published "La pampa . . . promesas" and "El hombre a la defensiva." He had returned to Buenos Aires in 1939 at the wrong time with the wrong message.

Add to that the resentment voiced in the "Epílogo para inglesses" that Ortega wrote in Paris in April 1938, and was included in all editions of *La rebelión de las masas* since then. There he forgets his ostensible impartially as he berates English intellectuals (collectively and anonymously as he had done with the Argentines) and, by extension, all leftward-leaning thinkers of the West, for having been duped in their support of the Spanish loyalists by "the Communists and their like" in Madrid. Albert Einstein, on the other hand, is singled out as a special target of the writer's wrath. The great physicist, it seems, had "assumed the right to express his opinion on the civil war in Spain and to take a position regarding it." [20] Whether the author of *La rebelión de las masas* ever pardoned Einstein for "this insolent interference" I don't know; but throughout his angry epilogue Ortega makes clear his authoritarian sentiments, lambasting liberals, pacifists and "internationalists" and declaring that only through "a phase of exacerbated nationalisms can the ultimate, concrete unity of Europe be achieved" (313).

It was in Buenos Aires in 1939 that Ortega was reported to have praised nationalist Spain's active ally, Benito Mussolini, as a statesman who combined "the lion's courage with the fox's shrewdness."[21] In the fall of that year he gave aseries of lectures, "El hombre y la gente" that he would later expand in a book under the same title. In the first of these lectures ("Ensimismamiento y alteración") he spoke lucidly on the perils of dehumanization in the contemporary world. History was definable as an uneasy alternation and synthesis of three "moments": existential loss of self in the growing confusion of things ("alteración"); being within oneself—*vita contemplativa* ("ensimismamiento"); and action based on a plan—*vita activa* ("praxis"). In this lecture he contrasted the ontological security of the tiger ("No matter what the tiger does, he can't stop being a tiger") with the mental and physical insecurity of the human being; we live—he says—in permanent danger of being dehumanized. In La Plata, also in 1939, he returned to the theme of young nations whose future is a question mark that he first enunciated in 1916. "Meditación del pueblo joven" the La Plata lecture in 1939) is noteworthy as a colonialist's justification of colonialization and its evolutionary consequences as he sees them—not the least of which is the paradoxical relationship he finds between *colonial existence* and *youthfulness*. "My subject is the young nation of colonial origin," he states, and outlines his disdainful theory in four points:

(1) Colonial life is a transitory phase in history that anticipates another, more advanced phase. By contrast, life in Asia, Europe, or ancient Greece is not transitory; "it ends in itself."
(2) Colonial life is "non-autochthonous." By definition it originated elsewhere.
(3) Colonization is an older nation's attempt to rejuvenate itself "in less civilized lands," or—in only slightly more comforting words for his New World readers, "historically younger."
(4) Colonial environments inevitably constitute "a regression to primitivism." (*MPJ*, 209–32)

The net effect of this point of view, this greening of sagacious Old World cultures in less civilized climes, could not have sat very well—as "El hombre a la defensiva" certainly didn't ten years before—with an expectant "young" Argentine audience that hungered for an uplifting message.

Undoubtedly, Ortega was reflecting on his own situation as a European outsider as much as to the twentieth-century status of the Americas, just as in another brief essay written the same year but published posthumously—"Balada de los barrios distantes"—he pictures himself as a distraught stranger near the corner of Corrientes and Florida being bumped aside by greedy shoppers "endowed with three necessary skills: audacity, rudeness and haste" (*MPJ*, 235). His sense of personal isolation coincided with the grim circumstances of Spain and Europe in 1939.

We should also remember that he was the victim of pirated editions of most of his works, especially in Chile, and that he and Victoria Ocampo had been entirely justified in publishing angry protests in November, 1937.[22] But while Ocampo was specific in her criticism, Ortega's retaliation encompassed a much broader spectrum of enemies. In addition to the fraudulent clandestine publishers, he attacked (again, naming no one) writers, intellectuals, and Latin Americans collectively. The pirate editors responsible were "Auracanian outlaws." The aggrieved author wondered "what Chilean intellectuals were made of" to make them accomplices in such an enterprise, and what had kept at least two hundred other Argentines from denouncing it before Victoria Ocampo had taken on the responsibility herself. Worst of all—he believed—the illegal editions reflected a deeper problem: "Excuse me for saying this, but the collective soul of Hispanic Americans is deeply mired in immorality." Ultimately, neither Ortega nor his ideological opponents in the "Alianza de Intelectuales de Chile para la Defensa de la Cultura" in their response—sent and probably written by Pablo Neruda—were willing or able to clarify the issue, and both parties showed a noticeable weakness in the skills of investigative reporting.[23] Ortega let his wrath rekindle a disdain for Hispanic Americans that had smoldered within him since his "Carta a un joven argentino que estudia filosofía" in 1925.[24] Neruda and his group used the situation to condemn the Spanish accuser for his "shameful silence" regarding the Spanish Civil War.

In conclusion, Ortega y Gasset's Argentine experience during his three stays between 1916 and 1942 reveals a progressive intellectual estrangement. He was not *independent* in his silent refuge as his country tore itself apart in a fratricidal war. Rather, he deluded himself into thinking he was neutral, despite the glaring bias exemplified by statements in "Epílogo para ingleses" and in Victoria Ocampo's monthly *Sur* on the pirated-editions controversy in 1937. By intensifying his colonialist assessment of Argentina and Hispanic America during his last stay in Buenos Aires he completed a process of alienation that had casually begun in the mid-1920s. The result was, as he declares in a November 1939 talk at the Institución Cultural Española de Buenos Aires (reproduced in *MPJ*, 193–207) his ultimate status as outsider and foreigner ("A foreigner! A man out of place, who just comes and goes"). Years before, in a pointed response to "El hombre a la defensiva," Emilio A. Coni had already labeled him an out-of-touch intellectual: "Foreign philosophers recently visiting

us have restricted their presence to the circle of listeners at their
lectures, believing that by dealing with them they would familiarize
themselves with Argentine thought. They couldn't be more mistaken."[25]

Ortega's political aloofness, which he testified to in a series of articles in *Crisol* of Buenos Aires in 1931, was perceptively criticized by
the young Enrique Anderson Imbert, who drew a pertinent parallel
between the intellectual elitism of Julian Benda (*La Traison des clercs*,
1928) and that of *La rebelión de las masas*, from 1930 on, Ortega's
most widely read work in Argentina. Politics, suggested Anderson
Imbert, was not a dirty activity to be ignored but a civic exercise that
called for proper civic control. Ortega he says, "causes us [in the
Crisol articles] with journalistic belligerence to wonder: What if political preoccupations were the true 'theme of our time'? What if politics were something we have to participate in—willingly or not?"[26]

To be sure, Ortega was consistent, and persistent, in his individualism. For him freedom was a strong-willed, first-person-singular
matter. But starting in 1930, his essays show that he paid for it with
isolation, a price that was ideological and cultural as well as personal. From the moment he sat down to write "Por qué he escrito
'El hombre a la defensiva'" (published in *La Nación* of Buenos Aires
on April 13, 1930), he was as much "a man on the defensive" as any
Argentine. There's no doubt that most Argentine readers sensed he
was looking at them askance. At best, their country and their literature were of superficially symbolic interest to him. To begin with he
did not read "American" works—or, if he did, chose not to deal with
them in writing. Further, he did not cultivate American intellectual
friendships, with two notable exceptions: Victoria Ocampo and Alfonso Reyes (with the latter only until 1932, when there seems to
have been a falling-out with him). Many of his contemporaries, including Pedro Henríquez Ureña, Amado Alonso, Ramón Gómez de
la Serna, Waldo Frank, Gabriela Mistral, and Alfonso Reyes—not to
forget Rubén Darío before them—and gone to Río de la Plata in the
spirit of sympathetic curiosity, and all found that they could teach
something and learn something at the same time. They gave to their
new relationships and surroundings what Ortega had called in one
of his early essays "un grado superior de atención."[27]

The month and year of Ortega's first arrival in Buenos Aires (July,
1916), an anonymous note appeared in the journal *Nosotros* that ex-

presses the magnitude of expectations that then existed—an ironic contrast to the mutual disillusionments in Argentina after that:

"Ortega has begun publication of *El Espectador*, a journal to which he'll be the sole contributor and is sure to reveal his profound culture. Will he offer impressions of our country like those he plans for Asturias and Castile? Will he write a new book? Few are as well prepared as Ortega to understand us. Maybe we'll soon have a foreigner's book that really penetrates the depth and complexity of our national character."[28]

No such book—we now well know—was destined to appear. The potential for it was not within Ortega's perspective, or his sensibility, or his temperament. Limited by his cultural colonialism, absorbed in his intellectual Narcissism, alienated from the Spanish Republic and, consequently, from the great majority of intellectuals in his era, he permanently misunderstood Argentina, the Argentines and—by extension—the New World. The same intensity of artistic vision that made him a great writer had the ultimate effect of weakening his perception of the modern world's conflictive realities.

6

Circling the Aleph: Short-Story Perspectives

A STORYTELLER'S TASK IS NOT LIMITED TO TELLING; IT ALSO CALLS FOR his or her participation. The Uruguayan Horacio Quiroga (1878–1937), like Eudora Welty, Gabriel García Márquez, and Jorge Luis Borges later on, preferred considering himself an invisible companion of the characters in his stories. Quiroga made that clear in his "Decalogue of the Perfect Story Writer" (1925) intended as a gift of advice to less experienced authors. In the last of its ten precepts he suggested: "Write as if your story were of interest only to the small circle of your characters—of which you might well have been one."

Years later Julio Cortázar (1914–83) published an essay of his own—"On the Short Story and its Circumstances" that begins with a quotation from what he considered Quiroga's indispensable precept (the first nine, by contrast, he placed in the "dispensable" category).[1] Cortázar was particularly interested in the phrase "of which you might well have been one." He wanted to emphasize the autonomy of fictional characters as the first requirement for a "great story," and compared the narrative process to an expanded soap bubble as it floats away from the author's clay pipe. As with the bubble, the invention of a character is his or her "liberation." Elaborating on the pipe-and-bubble metaphor, he says the *telling* and the *action* of the story become one. Most importantly, the narrative process is found "in the bubble, not in the pipe." To create a character is synonymous with setting it free, if not from predetermined circumstances, at least from the author's inevitable limitations.

So—combining Quiroga's concept of the narrator's double function (as both author and actor) with Cortázar's concept of the author as manipulator of conditions determined only by the characters and the characters' circumstances in the story—we can appreciate their creative potential and vitality, as well as the zone of mystery they're predestined to inhabit.

A good example of these functions is found in Ernest Hemingway's "The Killers." On a late afternoon two hired gunmen enter a
diner where most of the action will take place. In the course of their
pointedly uncordial conversation with George, who waits on custom-
ers at the counter, the sinister couple reveals its intention to kill Ole
Andreson, whom they expect to arrive in about an hour. The seri-
ousness of their plan is confirmed by their actions. While one of the
killers (Al) ties up the only other customer (Nick Adams) and the
cook in the kitchen, the other (Max) "instructs" George:

"If anybody comes in you tell them the cook is off, and if they
keep after it, you tell them you'll go back and cook yourself. Do you
get that, bright boy?"

"All right." George said. "What are you going to do with us after-
ward?"

"That'll depend," Max said. "That's one of those things you
never know at the time."[2]

Max's words ("*one of those things you never know at the time*") reflect
a major miracle of the art of story telling: a structural coincidence
between reality and fiction. As is often the case in everyday experience, the outcome of "The Killers" is foreseen. But no one—
including the author—is omniscient; no one can know the ultimate
details of its realization. Like his author and readers, Ole Andreson
is aware he'll be killed and accepts it as fact. But his death is not to
take place until after the story ends. We don't attribute the narrative
and artistic importance of "The Killers" to the consummation of
Ole's death, but—rather—to the emotion intensified by its inevitability and the tragic resonance that Hemingway makes us feel continuously—and which he shares, in the manner of an orchestra's
conductor with his characters (his musicians, so to speak) and his
readers (i.e., his audience).

Another narrative miracle is "A Worn Path" by Eudora Welty, like
William Faulkner, a native of Mississippi. The author has often received letters asking the same question about an unclear aspect of
her story; and the question is reiterated as the title of an essay (1974)
in which Welty responds to her readers' curiosity: "Is Phoenix Jackson's Grandson Really Dead?" Her response coincides with Quiroga's and Cortázar's statements in favor of autonomy for fictional
characters. The vital factor is a *trajectory*. That is, the "worn path" is
Phoenix Jackson's repeated route from her house in the country to
the doctor's office in town. She travels it often to get the medicine

needed for her ailing young grandson. When after several such trips the nurse on duty skeptically asks if the child might already be dead, Phoenix emphatically replies that he lives and will surely survive. According to the author, the question of the grandson's death or survival is of little artistic or literary consequence, and she declares: "My best answer would be: '*Phoenix* is alive.'" Then she adds: "The real dramatic force of a story depends on the strength of the emotion that has set it going. The emotional value is the measure of the reach of the story. What gives any such content to "A Worn Path" is not its circumstances but its *subject*: the deep-grained habit of love."[3]

Emotion is the driving force. Emotion (love, fear, joy, pain, rancor, compassion) complemented by the senses (the five elementary ones) is further enhanced by a metaphysical element, which can function as a hallucinatory spark. And of course, the imagination is always at work, often overflowing from dreams or the subconscious. Blake, Goya, and Borges have forcefully confirmed those connections.

As if anticipating the metamorphoses of Kafka and Cortázar, the Guatemalan Rafael Arévalo Martínez composed "El hombre que parecía un caballo" in 1914, which was published the following year. This memorable mobile portrait (literally and figuratively mobile) of Sr. de Aretal ("The Man Who Looked Like a Horse") was based on the author's impressions of an eccentric Colombian poet, Miguel Angel Osorio (1880–1942) who lived and wrote under three successive pseudonyms: Main Ximénez, Ricardo Arenales, and Porfirio Barba Jacob. The last of the three would become his permanent identity in literary history.[4]

The pseudonyms of Arévalo Martínez's "real-life" model could be considered a reflection of his fictional generic transition. The metamorphosis of a man into a horse is interesting both for its suggestive ambiguity and the neo-Baroque opulence that was often a characteristic of the poetic "modernism" (*modernismo*) widely practiced in Hispanic-American literature from about 1880 to 1915. Sr. de Aretal, who gallops off at the end of the story "with his human face and animal's body," is a mythical and modern centaur in the fullest degree. His quivers, his aloofness and his restlessness belong as much to a horse as to a "poet of inorganic verses." The equine-appearing man with the cocked head and long, hard limbs described in the first paragraph is also "el señor de los topacios": the topaz man of aristocratic demeanor and shallow convictions. With all his horsiness, he's still the poet who produces "a marvelous work of crystal tinged with its surrounding elements" and at the same time reflects the morbidity of an intellectually refined yet spiritually bereft artist who, when least expected by those around him, emits discreet whinny noises.

We should keep in mind that as well as an ingenious portrait of magical effects, "El hombre que parecía un caballo" is the vivid close-up of a literary relationship which includes a veiled self-portrait of Arévalo Martínez working as the ironic critic. According to his daughter and biographer (Teresa Arévalo), the author was especially proud of what he had written and on an October afternoon in 1914 decided to visit the horse/man model himself and read his creation to him. As might have been expected, Barba Jacob was not pleased with the performance. In his artistic enthusiasm Arévalo Martínez had offended him not only with his mockery of Barba Jacob's decadent *modernista style,* but also because the caricature had called attention—if only indirectly—to what appeared to be the protagonist's effeminate inclinations. Teresa Arévalo writes that as soon as her father finished his reading the Colombian poet quickly confessed his homosexuality and insisted that the story never be published. "It would fill me with shame, and you have no right to do it. Your narration is a breach of confidence."[5]

Jorge Luis Borges's story "El aleph" (1945) was a still more adventurous exercise of perspective. As in the case of "Él hombre que parecía un caballo," the author had three basic motives: a convergence of magic and reality, the caricature of a self-obsessed poet, and a parody of fashionable stylistic excesses (decadent *modernismo* in "El hombre . . . ," stilted academese in "El aleph"). The *instrumental* purpose in Borges's story is still more noticeable than in Arévalo Martínez's. "El aleph" is designed to expose a conflict of two literary personalities—Carlos Argentino Daneri and "Borges"—in a predestined situation, to satirize the literary environment of the early 1940s in Buenos Aires, and to specify by means of fantasy the author's concept of poetry's perceptive power—aided, of course, by a small kaleidoscopic device located in the basement of Argentino Daneri's house. First, as in "El hombre que parecía un caballo," "El aleph" describes an uncomfortable literary relationship. Borges (the narrator and very subjective protagonist) presents himself as shy, intuitive, and intensely lyrical. By contrast Carlos Argentino Daneri is verbose, pedantic, and anti-lyrical, traits abundantly confirmed in an endless poem (*La tierra*) that he insists on reading aloud to "Borges" with pompous explanations each time the latter visits (always on April 30, the birthday of Argentino's first cousin, Beatriz Viterbo, prematurely deceased).

The trio of Carlos Argentino Daneri, Beatriz Viterbo, and "Borges" constitutes a burlesque of their counterparts in *La Divina Commedia*. Argentino Daneri is a false literary descendant of Dante Alighieri (the first three and last three letters of "Daneri" form a contraction of Dante's first and second names). Beatriz Viterbo is a trivialized version—generously sugared in the narrator's memory—of Beatrice, the ideal beloved in *La Vita Nuova*. "Borges" is a reversal of Vergil's role as Dante's guiding spirit in *La Divina Commedia*. That is, in Dante's work Vergil leads the true poet through hell, purgatory, and earthly paradise, whereas in "El aleph" Daneri the myopic scribbler corners a passively Vergilian Borges each April 30 in his living room and manipulates him at will. "The Earth" in scrupulous detail (Argentino Daneri's condensation of Dante's paradise) is glimpsed *totally and simultaneously* in a small gyrating sphere (the Aleph). Daneri has invited his friend and literary rival downstairs to see it for himself; and what the character Borges discovers is author Borges's equivalent (under the stairs in Daneri's basement) of Dante's Paradise (viewed from a mountain top). To complete the irony, the author reveals in a postscript (*Posdata del primero de marzo de 1943*) his suspicion that what he saw or thinks he saw in the basement was "a false aleph."[6]

Keeping in mind another aspect of Borges's broad motivation in publishing "El aleph," we shouldn't forget Daneri's first *apellido: Argentino*. In the postscript just mentioned it's pointed out that Argentino Daneri won second prize ("el Segundo Premio Nacional de Literatura") for "a selection of Argentine pieces" from his interminable creation, and that Borges's own entry (*Los naipes del tahur*) got not a single vote from the awards committee.[7] Frieda Koeninger reminds us that the Daneri-Borges conflict in "El aleph" is a comical reflection on a literary quarrel that unfolded in Argentina in 1942 and 1943.[8]

The skillful satire of Carlos Argentino Daneri's passion for physical detail is a clear though indirect attack on the archaic tastes of Roberto F. Giusti and Alfredo A. Bianchi, coeditors of the journal *Nosotros* from its foundation in 1907 until 1943, when it ceased publication. In the context of Borges's comic opera Daneri sings the *buffo* part, meticulously echoing in his style Giusti's and Bianchi's dull preferences. By contrast Borges was then an editor of Victoria Ocampo's cosmopolitan monthly *Sur*, which was published from 1931 to 1971 and was everything *Nosotros* was not. He had a loftier, much more philosophical inclination than the nationalistic prize winners of 1942. He was a persistent experimentalist, and from the 1930s to the poetry of the last years was able to harmonize his own deeply Argentine nostalgias and ironies with appreciative readings of European and North American literature. He enacted the vitality of a new generation and realized a new vision.

Curiously, in chapter 21 of *The Western Canon* (1994), Harold Bloom chooses as the model for Carlos Argentino Daneri none other than Pablo Neruda, revealing in the process his unfamiliarity with literary life in Buenos Aires in the 1940s. Bloom calls Borges's story "a critique of poetic sprawl" and finds a considerable amount of such detail and verbosity in *Canto general.*[9] He's also aware of the natural disdain that Borges and Neruda felt for each other. The comparison of *Canto general* and "La tierra" is a tempting one, but Borges had other things in mind. To begin with, he wrote his parody in 1945 and published it in a book in 1949, still a year *before* the first edition of *Canto general* (1950). Further, the kind of sprawl found in "La tierra" is hardly "poetic" in Neruda's or Walt Whitman's vein— even at Neruda's and Whitman's worst. Quite the contrary, Daneri's output is *prosaic* sprawl of the kind favored by Giusti and Bianchi in the twilight year of *Nosotros*, and the Academia Argentina de las Letras of the same era, partisans all of the humdrum regionalism produced by Eduardo Acevedo Díaz, Jr. and César Carrizo, the first and second prize winners in 1942. Bloom's search for kindred spirits is appealing as an inventive exercise in comparative literature, but it misses the mark.

Of a different time and concern are the stories of Borges's compatriot, Luisa Valenzuela. In her *Cambio de armas* (1982) and *Donde viven las águilas* (1983) the will to liberation (that of women in several instances) frequently conflicts with the dark force of oppression experienced by victims and victimizers during the military rule in Argentina from 1976 to 1983. Action in the very brief "Los censores" (in *Donde viven las águilas*) unfolds in the sinister offices of the "Department of Censorship of the Ministry of Communications" (a most appropriate oxymoron for this plot) and in the pusillanimous conscience of Juan, the protagonist. Juan has received the new address of his friend Mariana, who is exiled in Paris, and quickly decides to write her. But as soon as he does, possible consequences begin to afflict him, the worst being the certainty of Mariana's abduction and disappearance if the Argentine authorities happen to intercept his letter. His preoccupation intensifies to the extent that he solicits and gets for himself a position as censor, his sole purpose being to retrieve the letter. His dedication to the job earns him a series of promotions in the department of censorship; from section K he moves up to section J, then from J to E. Later, after he acquires in the still more prestigious section B a reputation for "truly patriotic accomplishment" enhanced by his performance as "the perfect censor," Juan receives the returned letter. Valenzuela's conclusion leaves no doubt as to Mariana's fate: "As expected, he denounced her coldly. Also as expected, he could do nothing to prevent her execution at dawn. She became one more victim of his professional dedication."[10]

Juan and his steady moral descent are unmistakable and ironically described—from the outside—by the author. In Valenzuela's much longer "Cambio de armas" the relationship between victim and victimizer is revealed through the protagonist's dilemma and suffering as a captive: intimately, from the inside. That is, the story is told in an alternation of the explicit and the implicit from the viewpoint of Laura (or "the so-called Laura"). Accused of subversive activity, she has been detained and tortured and placed in the custody of her paramour, an army colonel of the same era in which "Los censores" takes place.

The Colonel has a steely-eyed look; he mistreats his mistress psychologically and verbally as well as physically; he shows no emotion—except, at the end, fear. His almost robotic performance lacks individuality, dedicated as it is to officially supported oppression. Laura's apartment is her prison, guarded round the clock by "One" and "Two," never seen but always out in the hall. The conditions of her confinement have also caused sporadic memory lapses and she frequently forgets the colonel's name (Roque), which is mentioned only once in the story—a possible symbol of his depersonalization? "The so-called Laura"—as if to say, her identity is diminished by her mistreatment—intermittently relives her past, including episodes of her sexual subjugation. She thinks her apartment, with only one window, is on the fifth or sixth floor, but isn't sure. The bedroom has a mirror on the ceiling, and when on one of several occasions of forced love-making he yells, "Open your eyes, slut! Confess. Tell me who your master is," she screams back at him, "No." It is, writes her author, "A *no* so intense, so profound, that it has no echo in their closed atmosphere, and he doesn't hear it; a *no* that seems to shatter the mirror on the ceiling, to multiply and mutilate and destroy his image, almost like a gunshot he doesn't notice; but both his image and the mirror remain there, intact and unperturbed."[11]

The end comes in accelerated form. The regime supported by the Colonel is being overthrown; he tells Laura he's escaping and she's free to go wherever she wants. We learn that her arrest occurred when she was seized in the act of trying to shoot him; and now, curiously, he leaves the same revolver in her possession as he heads for the door. The last sentence in the story is suggestive enough: "Now she raises it and aims."

In addition to her work as feminist critic, the Puerto Rican Rosario Ferré writes novels, poems, and stories. She shares Luisa Valenzuela's deep preoccupation for human rights, and several of her stories center on circumstances of a precarious sexual relationship. In "Cuando las mujeres quieren a los hombres" (in *Papeles de Pandora*, 1976), two very different ladies (one "of the night," the other of society) give their retrospective impressions of the deceased Ambrosio. The conditional symmetry of the tale is striking. Just as they shared Ambrosio's past, Isabel la Negra (his prostitute-lover) and Isabel Luberza (his high-society widow) will now share his inheritance on a fifty-fifty basis. A more trivial detail—their mutual fondness for a nail polish called Cherry Jubilee—adorns the symmetry and symbolizes a narrative convergence.

In their shared dilemma the two Isabels begin experiencing a strange mixture of hate and intimacy. "Ambrosio," of course, comes from *ambrosia*, defined in the Dictionary of the Spanish Royal Academy as "a substance that delights the spirit" and "any food, dish or drink of refined or delicate taste." He died a long time ago but is still—as fate would have it—an attraction, exerting an unforeseen influence on his two heirs. The figure that once divided the women has since his death motivated their coming together. Little by little each of the Isabels psychologically absorbs the other. Adding to the irony is a reversal of their respective economic fortunes: while the widow's part of the estate diminishes steadily, the mistress has prospered in spectacular fashion: to the extent that she proposes moving her house of prostitution from its low-class section of Ponce to the palatial residence still occupied by the widow.

"When Women Love Men" concludes with the two protagonists face to face. Isabel la Negra has paid her rival an unannounced visit with the purpose of reaching an accord. But with that confrontation the strange relationship between the two heiresses remains undefined, and as the story ends their accord—whether or not it's to be realized—is still pending.

In the prologue to his anthology of short stories, *El muro y la intemperie* (1989) Julio Ortega singles out two exemplary viewpoints for contemporary authors: Julio Cortázar's tends to be relativistic, while the Mexican Juan Rulfo's is fatalistic, "without alternatives."[12] To be sure, Cortázar and Rulfo are the best representatives of the two extremes.

In Rulfo's "El hombre," the man tracked along a riverbank over a period of uncounted days, then cornered and killed in a narrow canyon (*El llano en llamas*, 1953), is condemned from the start. His pursuer is following—literally—the man's footprints, and tells us in the second paragraph that the prospective victim's footprints in the mud reveal a missing big toe on his left foot and thus show his unmistakable path, easily distinguishable from the tracks of others. The plot is carried by the pursued and pursuer's alternating monologues and culminates in a shepherd's detailed testimony to a police official or lawyer on "the man's" harrowing experience (his fatigue, hunger, and thirst and, especially, his pangs of conscience for having killed an entire family—his pursuer and executor excepted—with a machete). He also describes the man's final disposition: face down in the river with the back of his neck full of bullet holes. A symbolic detail worthy of note (Rulfo's insinuation of providential justice?) is the missing left toe referred to above: the man lopped it off inadvertently as he hacked his victims with the machete.[13]

The Mexican and his machete have an important precedent in Horacio Quiroga's equally fatalistic "El hombre muerto," a five-page story in *Los desterrados* (1926). There the unnamed "man and his machete" are clearing out a section of a banana plantation in the Paraná valley. Here also the protagonist's left foot has an important function; it slips on a piece of bark fallen from a fence post and as the man falls the machete he has dropped penetrates his lower abdomen, mortally wounding him. Above the branches of the banana trees he can see the late morning sun reflected on the roof of his house and hear his little boy calling him, "Piapiá! Piapiá!" During the half hour it takes him to die he reflects on the "absurdity" of what has occurred and the strange stability of everything around him. "Nothing has changed. Only he is different." Two minutes ago he fell on the machete blade, and since then he has no more to do with his daily work routine, his family or his surroundings. "Since two minutes ago, he's been dying."[14]

Whereas Rulfo and Quiroga clarify in their narratives what has to be, Julio Cortázar offers ambiguous settings in which unexplainable hidden forces are at work. No one can explain, for example in "Axolotl," how the narrator's fixation on a larval salamander in an aquarium enables him to assume—progressively and completely over a series of visits—the imprisoned creature's viewpoint and identity. In most of Cortázar's stories we find a mixture of humor (especially jocular in the antics of his humanized little globules in *Historias de cronopios y de famas* [1962]) and a strange foreboding of evil or catastrophe.

In "Las babas del Diablo" (*Las armas secretas*, 1958) the camera competes, or conspires, with the narrative voices that complain about the difficulties of storytelling, Roberto Michel, a Franco-Chilean writer and amateur photographer, leaves his Parisian apartment on a November day. A couple (mother and son? probably not) on a park bench on the Quai de Bourbon attracts his attention and he makes numerous conjectures on their status and relationship. "I'm not describing anything; rather, I'm trying to understand."[15] Halfway through the story the photographer-narrator notices a man in a gray hat seated at the wheel of a car, either reading a newspaper or asleep. Shortly after he takes a picture of the couple (and the woman's angry demand that he give her the film) the man in the gray hat gets out of the car and approaches. He has white wrinkled skin, like a clown's, a crooked mouth, and black nostrils. At that point the scene abruptly changes to Michel's apartment as he develops and enlarges the disputed photo, which intimates some form of depravity. The story ends in the form of a nightmare or hallucination in which the three subjects of the photograph vividly reappear. The woman seems to be scolding or demanding something from the adolescent boy, as the clown-like man (now with a black tongue and black holes for eyes) quickly approaches the narrator. The "Devil's Drool" is all over the place.

It's important to note that Julio Ortega's division between a clear outcome and an ambiguous relativity is seldom absolute. In most cases the two tendencies complement each other. A good example is found in García Márquez's "Un hombre muy viejo con unas alas enormes" (1968). Between the humanized angel's or angelic human's crash landing in Pelayo and Elisenda's patio and his painful farewell flight, we're offered an impressive variety of endings, stimulated by the creative imagination and special interests of diverse local inhabitants: of the priest who will have to explain the phenomenon to his bishop, of ailing pilgrims in search of a healing miracle, of circus entrepreneurs, of Pelayo and Elisenda, the forlorn angel's hosts who put him on display at the village fair, charging admission at a profit substantial enough to finance the construction of a two-story mansion that had windows reinforced with iron grills to keep any future angels out. There are even "visionaries" who want to utilize him as a breeding model, "to establish on earth a species of sagacious winged men who would take charge of the universe."[16] A creature more of the local earth than of heaven, he contracted measles at the same time as Pelayo's and Elisenda's young son and in nocturnal deliriums "whined awkwardly, like an aged Norwegian." Earthly but not earthbound: in the end the old angel produces enough muscle power to rise from the garden mud and fly toward an unknown destination. García Márquez demonstrates here, as he does repeatedly in *Cien años de soledad,* how closely the details of magic occurrence, common reality and what people want to believe or reject can fit harmoniously together.

García Márquez's light-hearted miracles and Borges's metaphysical conjectures, Cortázar's fascination with hidden forces and Welty's and Hemingway's forebodings highlight in modern ways the creative ritual initiated and reportedly exercised over a thousand-and-one nights by Scheherazade (whose husband has promised to strangle her if she doesn't keep the process going). Of all literary functions, the short story is expected to be the most *concise,* an adjective meaning "brief in form but comprehensive in scope" in the felicitous definition of *The Random House Dictionary of the English Language.* Somewhere in his notebooks Henry James has noted that the "inclusion and confusion" of life contrasts with the "discrimination and selection" of art. Following his thought, one could say that the short story seeks out a specific case; it gets to the heart of the matter. It's the progressive illumination of a problem or subject. That's why its origin has often been attributed to the fable. Nevertheless, as several examples in this essay suggest, even the most discriminating and selective creations are the result of multiple circumstances, accidental occurrences, and a variety of collaborators.

7

As the Fly Spies: Hispanic-American Essays

En el principio fue la mosca.

—Augusto Monterroso

¿Espantáis la mosca? Ella vuelve.

—Alfonso Reyes

IT WAS NOT UNTIL THE SECOND HALF OF THE TWENTIETH CENTURY THAT readers, critics and—especially—*publishers* outside the Hispanic world began taking Spanish-American literature seriously. International interest grew as Nobel prizes were awarded to Gabriela Mistral, Miguel Angel Asturias, Pablo Neruda, Gabriel García Márquez, and Octavio Paz, all between 1945 and 1990. Of course, the "Boom" in narrative writing in that period was a major factor. Novels and poetry led the way, while essays attracted progressively less attention. One indicator of the generic disparity was the publication in 1997 of *Encyclopedia of the Essay* in a volume of over one thousand pages.[1] The encyclopedia includes twenty-one Hispanic-American essayists and, in addition to articles on regional and national representations of the form, eighteen kinds from *autobiographical* to *travel*.

A detail is worthy of note. In each of those eighteen categories the great majority of authors dealt with are English-speaking, either from Great Britain or the United States. Further, in *not one* of the articles on said categories is a Hispanic-American author mentioned, let alone commented on. To be sure, across the centuries since Michel de Montaigne, the essay has found its most comfortable home in England and her powerful ex-colony; and the genre is thought of as more in harmony with a venerated, slower-moving past than the accelerated, anxious present. Graham Good complains that "the 'image' of the essay, when not stuck in the classroom, seems to be stuck in the Edwardian period, neglecting its great importance as an expression and vehicle of Modernism: Yeats, Eliot, Woolf, Lawrence, Forster, Pound."[2] True. But except in his bibliographical notes, Professor Good himself diminishes the genre's "immense importance" by limiting it in the ten chapters of his *The Observing Self* to the English-speaking reading-and-writing world.

Toward the end of the nineteenth century and throughout the twentieth, the essay in all literatures found a kind of parasitic refuge, infiltrating numerous other forms: the theater, meditative poetry, the novel, new- and old-style journalism, biography, criticism, interviews on- and off-camera. Does this help explain the dwindling critical interest in the form? Lionel Trilling's large anthology, *Experience of Literature* (1967), contains no essays; and long before, in their *Theory of Literature* (first edition, 1942) René Wellek and Austin Warren chose not to discuss the form—neither in chapter 10 ("Literature and Ideas"), nor in chapter 17 "Literary Genres").

But no matter; as if in response to these signs of indifference, Phillip Lopate wrote a piece for *The New York Times Book Review*, published November 18, 1984) entitled "The Essay Lives—in Disguise." In disguise, and in diffusion, we should add; and it really has always been that way. Shakespeare's most revered tragedy, as Robert Atwan has pointed out, cannot be considered an essay in dramatic form, but "Hamlet's mind undeniably works in an essayistic fashion. In speech after speech, we can hear Shakespeare responding to Montaigne's newly-formed genre."[3]

Although Hispanic American and other essays have been overlooked as a major genre and relegated by *The New York Times Book Review* and bookstore shelf labels everywhere to the fuzzed category of "non-fiction," their *function* persists. Diffusion has not resulted in extinction. The essay has found its place (sometimes provisional, sometimes truly vital) in other forms. Since the mid-twentieth century many academics under a structuralist or poststructuralist influence have tended to underestimate it—partly because of a desire to replace traditional concepts of reality with a system of signs, thereby transforming the anthropocentric world into an abstract linguistic universe. The result, maybe unintentional, was a literary dehumanization that far exceeded the modest apprehensions of Ortega y Gasset (*La deshumanización del arte*) in 1925. Almost by definition their semiotic concept precluded the essay: it saw writing as a system of signs designed to illuminate other signs. These "other" signs ultimately show that every object operates only as a "signifier." According to Jacques Derrida, that's all there is. Every word signifies but, paradoxically, there's nothing to be signified. "There's no such place as outside the text," he declares.[4]

Derrida's claim was certainly coherent; but if the imagination is more than a simple plaything and reality exists beyond that theorist's barbed wire enclosure of language, he and his like-minded colleagues were on an arbitrary and suicidal course to begin with, one that required an elimination of individuality and sucked the physical universe into a manageable abstraction. The essay has not accepted this arbitrary confinement to a world of signs. It has not made the required conceptual leap from language as a manifestation of reality to reality as a manifestation of language. In preserving its personal motivations it has saved its essential character. Significantly, structuralists and neostructuralists are seldom essayists themselves, because their passion for theoretic "discourse" has resulted in a sacrifice of the essayist's inherent aesthetic and intellectual *independence.*

As against other obstacles, the creative essay has successfully resisted these restrictions. Its unfashionable status among critics, theorists and profit-motivated publishers has not resulted in a loss of appeal to anonymous readers. It's pleasing to note that even some theorists, including the twentieth century's most intelligent semiotician—Umberto Eco—have remained uninhibited by poststructuralist concerns as they overtly exercise their imaginative powers. Eco is also a novelist and, as he demonstrates in his superb *Travels in Hyperreality* (American edition, 1986), an accomplished essayist. For Eco "signs are not only words, or images; they can also be forms of social behavior, political acts, artificial landscapes. As Charles S. Peirce once said, 'A sign is something by which we know something more.'"[5]

That "something more" (attention, Derrida) is the Hispanic-American essayist's true initiative and power. Think of José Martí and Gabriela Mistral, morally driven educators with lyric visions; Victoria Ocampo and Jorge Luis Borges, cosmopolitan enlighteners; José Vasconcelos, the temperamental revolutionary; Augusto Monterroso with his quirky fables in *La oveja negra y demás fábulas* (1969) and just as quirky commentaries in *Movimiento Perpetuo* (the published abode of Monterroso's magical fly, 1972); Julio Cortázar the humanizing ironist in *Historias de cronopios y de famas* (1962); Elena Poniatowska and the echoes of hidden realities in *La noche de Tlatelolco* (1971) and *Nada, nadie* (1988). The fact that both Monterroso's and Cortázar's creations are presented in a narrative format doesn't diminish their essayistic vigor. I believe literary history will see the essay's postmodern eclipse mainly as an academic illusion that cannot be blamed only on an élite of French critics whose influence—in both the intensity and extent of their semiological system—was doomed to evaporate circa 1980. Neither does scholarly indifference or lack of bookstore shelf space suffice as an explanation. The essay has survived because—as in all literature—inner functions overcome outside deterrents. Essayists abhor a vacuum. They flaunt or sneak personality into their work and revel in their thematic and imagistic freedom, blissfully immune (like Cortázar's cronopios) to the theoretic viruses floating around them.

An insect analogy (inspired by Monterroso's first piece in *Movimiento perpetuo*—"Las moscas") is now appropriate. Metaphorically, essay writers duplicate the powers of the consistently disdained yet most versatile of all fauna: the common fly. Every writer seeks out and in some way exploits the fly's potential. Like García Márquez's endearing short-story protagonist—the old man with angel wings who shows he can be in several rooms of Pelayo's and Elisenda's house at the same time—the *musca domestica* has wings that make it magically ubiquitous. Intensive wide-angle sight enhances the scorned creature's confrontations—both stationary and aerial—with space and time. God or nature made fly-eyes extra large and spherical, like supersensitive telescopic and microscopic turrets, facilitating vision in all directions, as well as the ability to dodge in a hundredth of a second the hand or swatter aimed at crushing it. A writer's broad scope of possibilities is the true equivalent of what the fly's marvelous ocular instruments can bring to view, especially to the essay writer. In the negative sense, flies and essayists are traditionally under-appreciated and considered potentially disruptive. They get no critical respect; their agilities are confused with their trivialities. In a more positive sense, flies and essayists are the least predictable of all beings. In the spirit of *musca domestica* and in clear defiance of publishing companies, the essay has functioned more freely in Hispanic America. That has been the case despite a general refocusing of reader attention during the age of "The New Narrative" that blossomed in the 1960s.

In Hispanic America the genre's diversity of form has entailed what some would call an excessive freedom of definition. A lot of attention has been given to something too easily classified by literary scholars as essay, lumped together with academic lectures, close (and *closed*) critical analyses, "pensamiento," "estudios histórico-sociológicos," "socio-literatura" and other such terms found in Alberto Zum Felde's expansive grab bag, *Indice crítico de la literatura hispanoamericana: el ensayo y la crítica* (1954). An anthology edited in Mexico by Ernesto Mejía Sánchez, *El ensayo actual latinoamericano* (1971), is symptomatic of this heterogeneous view and includes, together with Concha Meléndez's sensitively symbolic prologue to her *Signos de Iberoamérica*, Alfredo L. Palacios's historically relevant but quite unliterary "Bolívar y Alberdi: comunidad regional iberoamericana." The introduction to Martin S. Stabb's book, *In Quest of Identity* (1967), comments on the Hispanic-American intellectual's many-sidedness and the frequent confluence of political and academic concerns in the writers' minds. Stabb prudently limits his attention to one kind of discursive prose, "the Spanish American essay of ideas," thus avoiding a frequent tendency among other New World scholars to call anything an essay that's not easily identifiable as a short story or novel. Also encouraging was the appearance in 1976 of José Luis Gómez-Martínez's semi-annual bulletin *Los Ensayistas,* which carried during the seven years of its publication a useful bibliography entitled "El ensayo como género literario." Gómez-Martínez also published *Teoría del ensayo* (2nd edition, 1992) which includes a useful discussion (chapter 20) of the relationship between the essay and other forms.[6]

The continual oscillation between strict and flexible classifications of the genre has been unsettling both to critics and creative writers—especially to the latter, who have tended to include (sometimes inadvertently, sometimes by design) essay-like passages in novels, short stories, or plays. There's little doubt that in most of the western world of the nineteenth and early twentieth centuries—times more favorable to letter-writing and, generally, prose in the representational vein—the essay was more at home. Times and circumstances, that is, in which conscious, authorial *pursuit of meaning* through a singular, subjective viewpoint found fuller acceptance, when irony was esteemed as much as ambiguity, and dialectic purpose as much as linguistic design.

But creative subversion underlies every writer's individuality, which is why there will always be essays. This is true, in part, because *commitment* (to a principle or ideal, not to a doctrine, party line, or convention) is always a stimulus in the writer's art. In an illuminat-

ing passage of his article "El ensayo hispanoamericano y su naturaleza" Juan Loveluck refers to the genre's "instrumental notes" (like
ideological combat, moral denunciation, testimony in adversity, and
circumstantial definitions of culture).[7] He then quotes from Leopoldo Zea's *América en la historia* (1957) to explain the phenomenon: "It's the concern of a man who wants to be more than the
reflection or echo of a culture, of a man who wants to take an active
part in it." A certain militancy, or at least acknowledgement of a
need for commitment has had positive effects, because it has given
the author's work idealistic vigor—as in the cases of Domingo Faustino Sarmiento, José Vasconcelos and, especially, José Martí. Without irony, ambiguity or much "wit," Martí is one of relatively few
prose writers who have successfully translated simple moral conviction into a complex art of the senses. To be sure, his sensitivities as
a poet made that possible. His voice—always *his* voice—echoes
through the castles of his imagery; and he was a spokesman for Hispanic America's main needs as well as a consummate instrumental-
ist. The last term is particularly appropriate in Martí's case, for his
prose was as musical as his verse.

Vasconcelos operated in a similar way, although stylistic crafts-
manship meant less to him. I'm referring to the Vasconcelos of *La
raza cósmica* (1925), *Indología* (1926), and his memoir *Ulises Criollo*
(1935) with its vividly reflective passages, not the Vasconcelos who
from about 1940 lapsed into a kind of ideological senility that con-
tradicted most of what he had advocated before. Ethical energy in
his best works gave him great power and made even his wildest theoretic vagaries in *La raza cósmica* interesting to read.

José Enrique Rodó, who at the dawn of the twentieth century
dreamed of a rarefied cultural aristocracy, was (like Vasconcelos) of
one mind and one voice. He envisioned a kind of second Renais-
sance, which would evolve on a new continent in the clouds: a land
in which important people would spend most of their time meditat-
ing in quiet rooms. Rodó's view—like a camera without a wide-angle
lens—missed too much of the real world's panorama. His writing
struck many readers as too far removed from humanity's everyday
problems. Did he grow old too fast? He was just twenty-nine when
Ariel (his only famous work) was published in 1900, and when his
style was set for the rest of his life. Granted, Rodó's essays and para-
bles are still important cultural reference points, but many of them
would seem archaic or obsolete in an anthology of living literature.

Then there was the embittered witness, possibly the most self-consuming of Hispanic-American essayists to date, Ezequiel Martínez Estrada, who combined a symbolist's obsession, manifested in his system of historical, geographic and topographic allusions, with a tragic sense of life—especially in *Radiografía de la pampa* (1933). One wonders if Borges had him in mind when writing the epilogue to *El hacedor*, in which a man engaged in drawing a map of the planet discovers shortly before dying that the intricate maze of lines reveals an image of his own face. Like Borges, Martínez Estrada tells us the self is a microcosmos, and the world a set of mirrors in which a failed hero reads his fate. But—unlike Borges—he chooses his failed heroes from among real writers (Sarmiento, William Henry Hudson, Martí, Nietzsche, Kafka) and reads their fate for them. The result, in each case, is a testimony of shared disillusionment.

Regarding Leopoldo Zea's explanation of the Hispanic-American idea of intellectual commitment, a disadvantage or literary handicap, so to speak, could be pointed out. The problem is exemplified by three of the authors just mentioned, who wrote in atmospheres of social and political turmoil. In older, colonial and nineteenth-century traditions "literature" was usually considered peripheral, a form of pastime. Poetry and the romantic novel centered on the writer's personal preoccupations and seldom dealt with collective or historical problems. A basic change began at the turn of the nineteenth and twentieth centuries, when many of the New World's intellectuals, including Martí, Vasconcelos, and, later, Martínez Estrada, assumed a more combative role. Enrique Anderson Imbert has observed that "up to 1890 intellectuals and the bourgeois walked together, in a spirit of cooperation. They were the architects and builders of our nations. But after 1890 the good relationship deteriorated."[8] Individually, intellectuals were respected, but as a group they had lost influence. But that change was really the result of a cultural preoccupation that started with the Spanish conquests of the early sixteenth century.

"Original sin" is what H. A. Murena called the disadvantage in his book *El pecado original de América* (1954), referring to the misfortune of having been born in Latin America. In literature and art, as well as in social and political doctrine, an enigma has emerged: the question of historical self-definition. One is tempted to think that in this context the essay from Sarmiento's *Facundo* (1845) to Paz's *Laberinto de la soledad* (1950) constituted a thematic divergence from the mainstream of literature, but it wasn't. José Hernández's *Martín Fierro*, novels of the Mexican Revolution, the short stories of Horacio Quiroga and Baldomero Lillo, Rubén Darío's *Canto a la Argentina* and the expatriate perspective of virtually all his prose and poetry, the fatalistic view in José Eustasio Rivera's and Rómulo Gallegos's novels and later in the historical ironies of Alejo Carpentier, Carlos Fuentes, García Márquez, and Vargas Llosa, not to forget Pablo Neruda's *Canto general* and Ernesto Cardenal's *Estrecho dudoso*, are convincing examples of how the New World concept of original sin has infiltrated every genre.

Within the essay itself an inhibitive process was at work: the Americanizer *as essayist* seemed to have worn out the relatively few nonfictional techniques left to his or disposal; all the variations on Martí's *Nuestra América* theme appeared to have been played out. For essayists in the skeptical twentieth century metaphoric freedom became more and more limited. Martí's exuberance (the new Adam naming everything in a new world) was missing. From his *Escenas norteamericanas* of the 1880s and 1890s to Paz's *El laberinto de la soledad* in 1950 there was a creative confidence that reflected authors' underlying conviction that conscientious exercise of their art would earn them a degree of self-deliverance and, by empathy, a corresponding self-deliverance for their readers. This was also true of the great essayists in Europe and the United States from Emerson and Thoreau to Nietzsche and Unamuno.

The dispersion and displacement of the essay (by reader preference, that is) during the late twentieth century could be explained in semantic terms. At the beginning of his article "Semantics,"[9] Donald Kalish refers to W. V. Quine's theories of "reference" and "meaning."[10] Quine distinguishes between symbols that function as denotation and *ex*tension (*reference*) and those others that function as connotation and *in*tension—i.e., intensification—(*meaning*).

A literary analogy to Quine's reference-meaning concept could be made. That is, most genres in most historical periods undergo a gradual movement from the pleasures of reference (the joy of naming, discovery, awareness of adventure, expectant viewpoints) toward the complexities of meaning (encounters with ambiguity, immanent allusions, epistemological experience, ironic viewpoints). In the *reference* phase the author's vision is outward; in the *meaning* phase it is inward. The movement from reference to meaning has nothing to do with "progress," development, or with aesthetic or ethical evaluations. It's more a question of attitude and mood; and the basic trend is from expectation to skepticism. It also follows a cycle of organic maturation, like the succession of four seasons. In that sense the Hispanic-American essay of the last third of the twentieth century, could be placed in late autumn. If its most of its leaves (signs) of meaning fell then, it could still anticipate a new beginning, its springtime of reference. Meanwhile—like all perennials—it hibernated.

Hibernation, of course, is suspended life, a reminder but never the metaphor of death. In Hispanic-American literature the term has additional significance: hibernation becomes a metaphor for one of the three states of the New World essay under discussion.

1. The first, already mentioned, is found in the Americanist prose of Martí, Rodó, Vasconcelos and Martínez Estrada. It amounted to an intermittent, cultural declaration of independence from the rest of the Western World. The second, nearly omnipresent, is the essay as hibernation, or absorbed species, whose main habitat is that of other genres. The third, less prevalent yet the most memorable, is the autonomous essay.

2. The hibernation essay is common to a wide variety of narrative works, either as an aggregate, quite explicit form, or as infiltrating, subsidiary pieces. An example of the explicit kind is one of Ernesto Sábato's innumerable meditations in *Abaddón el exterminador* (1974), in which a character had been asked "why we Latin Americans have great novelists but no great philosophers," and replied: "Because we're barbarians, . . . because fortunately we avoided the great rationalistic schism. Just as other peripheral ones—the Russians, the Scandinavians, the Spaniards—did. If you're looking for our *Weltanschaung*, try our novels, not our treatises of pure thought."[11] The infiltrating type is found in Rosario Ferré's *Eccentric Neighborhoods* (1999), a novel with many autobiographical reflections that incorporates commentaries on the Spanish-American War (1898), the Socialist Party, the possibilities of statehood, and all the cultural crosscurrents that affected Puerto Rican history and family life in the twentieth century.[12] Awareness of social and economic disparities is as vital in her story as it is in the essays of Martí, Ariel Dorfman (*Patos, elefantes y heroes*, 1985) or Eduardo Galeano (in the three volumes of *Memorias del fuego*, 1982–86), or in the novels of Luis Rafael Sánchez, García Márquez, or Isabel Allende. Ferré's "eccentric" neighborhoods include the shacks in which sugar cane workers and

their families slept eight to a room and the palatial residences in which the narrator's affluent family lived. One of the narrator's uncles, Tío Alejandro, the pampered son and heavy-drinking heir to his father's fortune, sold the family's sugar mill and farms and a year later bought a fifty-three-foot Chris Craft Sports Fisherman. On a memorably clear day, on his quest of "the biggest marlin of all" off the north coast of Puerto Rico, he was unceremoniously dragged into the ocean, possibly by that very fish on his hook, and never found. Historical memory is equally important in *Tinísima* (1992), Elena Poniatowka's biographical novel on the life of photographer and militant leftist Tina Modotti. It traces her agitated life and multiple contacts in the United States, Mexico, the Soviet Union, and Spain during its civil war. Hibernating essays also abound in Borges's stories in the form of speculations on infinity and numbers—for example—in "La biblioteca de Babel" and "El libro de arena—as well as in his ideas on the sense of perspective and space in poetry in "El Aleph."

Undoubtedly, incitement to infiltration has also come from notable autonomous essays in several literatures, such as Jonathan Swift's (not very) "Modest Proposal for Preventing the Poor People of Ireland from Being a Burden to their Parents or Country; and for Making Them Beneficial to the Publick." (1729), the kind of satire that also appears in the lottery-conducted-by-children episode in García Márquez's novel *El otoño del patriarca*. The same movement (from idea to fiction or poetry) can develop within a single author's opus. For example: Miguel de Unamuno's concepts of the crises of faith and rationality in *Del sentimiento trágico de la vida* (1913) are reiterated in his novel *San Manuel Bueno, mártir*, and Octavio Paz's theoretic assimilation of Tantric doctrine in his essays *Conjunciones y disyunciones* (1969) had been creatively applied two years earlier in his complex poem *Blanco*.

3. Finally, despite its overshadowing by other forms, the autonomous essay is still the basic "nonfictional" genre. It remains the one most carefully controlled by its author, and most likely to convey a discreet balance of experience and imagination; to maintain its quest of synthesis, i.e., to see things whole through their images and symbols; and to exercise effective persuasion on any of the diverse intellectual levels where the author openly solicits the reader's collaboration. Of course, fashion has not favored the major practitioners since the mid-twentieth century.

Nevertheless, their work survives—even if several classic essayists like Alfonso Reyes, the purest composer of the form in Hispanic America to date, is scarcely remembered except in small academic circles. Reyes was a lucid seer and his world is illuminated by a crystalline style, especially in *Visión de Anahuac* (1915) and *Ancorajes* (a collection of short pieces written between 1928 and 1948). He is spiritually *present* in all he writes, as James Willis Robb has persuasively shown.[13] Think also of Reyes's compatriot Julio Torri, and his ironic miniessays in *Ensayos y poemas* (1917) and *De fusilamientos* (1940). "De fusilamientos," the two-page title piece of the latter work, was written in 1915 in the heat of the Mexican Revolution, and Torri handles the issue of capital punishment with astute refinement, noting that public executions are inevitably vulgar, and that their spectators tend to be of "humble origin, rough sensibilities, and deplorably poor artistic taste." The Venezuelan Mariano Picón-Salas is also a case in point: his aesthetic appreciations in *Gusto de México* (1952), his historical perspectives in *De la conquista a la independencia* (1944) and *Intuición de Chile y otros ensayos* (1935), and the lucid reminiscences in his memoir *Regreso de tres mundos* (1959).

The form has also been skillfully practiced by novelists—notably Carlos Fuentes and Mario Vargas Llosa—and poets, famous for their work in verse, yet insufficiently appreciated for their essays: Gabriela Mistral's *Recados contando a Chile* (1955) and Pablo Neruda's *Una casa en la arena* (1966), recollections—mostly in prose—that could also be classified as poetry. Also largely overlooked: Rubén Darío's literary criticism in *Los raros* (1896) and *Letras* (1909), contemporary impressions in *Peregrinaciones* (1901) and *Todo al vuelo* (1912), speculations on dreams in *El mundo de los sueños* (published posthumously in 1917) and personal recollections in *La vida de Rubén Darío escrito por él mismo* (1914).

The most accomplished poet-essayist of the century was, indisputably, Octavio Paz, starting with his view of Mexican sensibilities in the first edition of *El laberinto de la soledad* (1950) and continuing with *El arco y la lira* (1956; 2nd ed., 1967), *Posdata* (1969) and *Tiempo nublado* (1986), and *Sor Juana Inés de la Cruz y las trampas de la fe* (1982) among others. His historical intuitions of the end of the modern era have gained validity since he wrote them. With poetic foresight he kept pace with the world in its dizzying spiral toward the unknown; from antiquity to our time traditions and systems merged with chaos, and out of chaos grew a new kind of collective solitude:

> "The stars were no longer the image of cosmic harmony. The center of the world was displaced, and God, ideas and essences were lost. We were left alone. The form of the universe changed, and man's view of himself changed; nevertheless, worlds were still the world, and men were essentially man. Everything was part of a whole. But now, space expands and disintegrates; time has turned discontinuous; the world, the whole, bursts into fragments. It's a dispersion of man, drifting in a space that also drifts, lost in its own dispersion."[14]

Dispersion of man; dispersion of the space he inhabits and meditates; dispersion—we could add—of the literary forms he writes in.

From Montaigne to Ortega y Gasset and Paz, essayists have been noticeably modest in appraising their art, which is probably a good thing. Ortega, to be sure, gave us a succinct definition, calling the essay "*la ciencia, menos la prueba explícita*" ("science, without explicit proof") and the phrase caught on, like a line from a popular song. Precisely because of its widespread acceptance as an axiom, it's important to realize that Ortega's concept was wrong, as these two images of the fly (A and B) suggest:

1. Let symbol A represent the common fly in the exacting perspective of science and (as with the word *ciencia* in Spanish) the broader context of general knowledge.[15]
2. Let symbol B represent the common fly in the flexible perspective of literature.

    The lines *converging* on the fly in symbol A reflect the inward movement of most scientific deductions and philosophical conclusions; the thinker zeroes in on the object of some search or investigation in order to place it in a system.

    The lines *diverging* from the fly in symbol B reflect the outward movement of most literary thoughts and visions. Science isolates and defines; its purpose is to find the fly (*musca domestica*) its appropriate function in nature or the universal order of things. Science tends to objectivity; its main context is system. Literature, by contrast, assimilates and fancifully selects; its purpose is to seek out and exploit the metaphorical potential of the fly (*musca poetica*)

Ortega y Gasset would have us believe that the essay is truncated science—a form of thought with the "proof" cut off. But *proof* is really irrelevant; it's the element of least importance in literature. Ortega leaves us adrift by failing to replace the eliminated element in his dictum (proof) with something else. Granted: science and literature can have similar or even identical initiatives. They both ask fundamental questions; but while the questions of science lead to appropriate and definitive answers, those of literature are asked in the deep premonition that such answers are not to be found. Literature does borrow and put to dynamic use a variety of scientific concepts: "Big Bang" as the origin of numbers, Darwin's ideas on natural selection, the infinity of numbers, Einstein's concept of space-time, the third law of thermodynamics, etc. But it is not founded on them. As Lionel Trilling points out, "when we speak of the relationship of literature and ideas, the ideas we refer to are not those of mathematics or symbolic logic, but only such ideas as can arouse and traditionally have aroused the feelings."[16]

One is tempted to reconstruct Ortega's definition—possibly as follows: "The essay is an idea, *plus* its fanciful development."

Ortega, wherever you are, would you approve of such a revision for the ultimate edition of *Meditaciones del Quijote*? Probably not. Individual definitions aside, the essay has always needed reconsideration. Precisely because it's still usually relegated to the trash heap of nonfiction (a passive nondefinition), it deserves revaluation. In that regard Alfonso Reyes has already been helpful. In "Apolo o de la literatura" (the third essay of *La experiencia literaria*) he distinguishes clearly between literature and science by contrasting "a scientific proposition" ("Heat expands masses")—that is, an established phenomenon in conformity with natural law—with "a poetic proposition" ("Like an oriental king, the sun expires"). The reality of the sunset, he points out, is unimportant to the reader; the poet's allusion to it is what counts. "Literature, a practical lie, is psychologically true."[17]

Like a poem or story, the essay retains an image or suggestion of reality, but at the same time it departs from reality in search of the infinite associations that create the imaginary event. Essayists from Montaigne to Reyes and Monterroso—and of course the indomitable fly—have made that clear.

8
Spain's Edgy Generation (1898)

> History is the action and reaction of these two—Nature and Thought; two boys pushing each other on the curbstone of the pavement.
>
> —Ralph Waldo Emerson, "Fate"

GENERATION IS A CIRCUMSTANTIAL TERM. LIKE *MOVEMENT, PERIOD, TREND,* or *era,* the word suggests a relationship that encompasses ideological accord and discord and, usually, a sharpened awareness of historical change, whether the change is felt as only impending or as one already in process.

Was there really a "Generation of 1898" in Spain? All considered, one concludes that there probably was, even though the question of its existence, nonexistence or semi-existence is still a persistent motive for debate. In my view, the disagreements themselves are the best evidence of the generation's continuing resonance and vitality. Although its writers seldom coincided in their points of view, they expressed a similar intensity in their cultural judgments and in their tendency to dissent from traditional interpretations.

Ricardo Gullón argues that the Spanish writers who were active in the late nineteenth and early twentieth centuries had too little in common to form a generation: "I fail to see how one could conceive of an ideological pattern, still less a political program, that included Unamuno's messianic compulsions, the bedroom-slipper 'anarchism' of Pío Baroja, Antonio Machado's softened Jacobinism, and Azorín's conservatism with authoritarian sentiments" (*La invención del 98 y otros ensayos* [Madrid, 1969]).

It's also true, as María de Maeztu observes, that Baroja, Unamuno, and Ramiro de Maeztu did not believe it existed (see her *Antología— Siglo XX*, Madrid, 1948). But she points out that Baroja in a lecture given in 1926 ("Tres generaciones") qualified his view by stating that a "Generation of 1870" (i.e., of writers born in or near that year) did exist, Maeztu also quotes José Ortega y Gasset, who in "La idea de las generaciones," the first chapter of *El tema de nuestro tiempo* (1923) defines the phenomenon as "a human variety" to be classified following "an equation" determined by two elements: "what is received" and "what is spontaneous." The tension created by those opposing elements is the nucleus of a generation. Ortega specifies two kinds of historical environment in which a generation develops. One shows a relatively harmonious balance between its "received" influences and its "spontaneous" urges toward self-expression (*épocas cumulativas*). In the other, traditional ideals and values are questioned and often rejected (*épocas eliminatorias y polémicas*). Older thinkers and writers recollect more and tend to prevail in "cumulative" eras. Younger, more experimental and provocative thinkers and writers set the tone in "polemical" times.

Also pertinent to a generation's creative vision is the duality discussed by Ortega in chapter 6 of the same work ("Las dos ironías, o Sócrates y Don Juan"). That is, the conflict between "pure reason" and "spontaneity."[1] The last sentence of his essay declares: "*Pure reason must yield its empire to vital reason.*" The statement reflects its author's recognition of the *biological* element operative in the Don Juan legend across several centuries of Spanish culture. Were the writers of the Generation of 1898 enacting their own quest of this Vital Reason? Nowhere in *El tema de nuestro tiempo* does Ortega name one of them as an example, notwithstanding his own interest in the idea of intellectual generations. "Vital reason," after all, was a basic ingredient of the modernist trend that affected literature, politics, and religion in Europe and all the Americas at the turn of the nineteenth and twentieth centuries. The wide-ranging effects of the phenomenon also help explain Gullón's criticism of Azorín's "invention" of the Generation of 1898 in an essay in 1912. He prefers the broader classification of an intercontinental Hispanic modernism, which—it should be recalled—began in the 1880s with the Hispanic American poetry and prose of José Martí, Rubén Darío, and José Asunción Silva. Hispanic modernism, as Gullón perceives it, is also animated by the polemical spirit of Unamuno and his peninsular contemporaries.

Indeed, the most representative Spanish authors, circa 1900, formed an integral part of modernism, a trend that embraced three important developments of that era: (1) the aesthetic innovations (in large part those of Martí, Darío, and Silva) in Hispanic-American literature; (2) the much broader circumstances in Europe and the West of literature affected by historical and technological change, such as the forces of revolution, new methods of warfare, the development of automation, electronics, internal combustion, powered flight, etc.); and (3) the liberalizing movement within Christianity denounced by Pope Pius X in his Encyclical of 1907.

Modernism expressed itself architecturally as well, first with the Eiffel Tower, later with skyscrapers in New York and several other cities. The Eiffel Tower (1889), built for the Universal Exposition of Paris, was the movement's foremost symbol. The tower was not a building in the utilitarian sense, or a monument, or a religious structure. Its function as a tourist attraction was secondary to its aesthetic implications. It anticipated the nonconformist spirit of the Generation of 1898 and those writers' basic desire to surpass a fastidious present. The structure's emphatic height and absence of usable spaces constituted an open if skeptical question mark. What levels of achievement—scientific, religious, or artistic—could humanity now aspire to, and with what purpose?

Politically, the generation's writers expressed their modernism through a combination of cultural impatience and disappointment with current events. The doctrines of Mikhail Bakunin and Prince Peter Kropotkin, two aristocrats with revolutionary sentiments, were well known in Spain, where the government, the people and the intelligentsia were attempting to sidestep the land mines of anarchism. Together with their soon-to-be North American opponents in war, Spaniards absorbed the psychological shockwaves from the sinking of the battleship Maine on February 15, 1898. Another of the preludes to the "Disaster" (Spain's word for their quick loss two months later of Cuba, Puerto Rico, and the Philippines) was the assassination of Prime Minister Antonio Cánovas del Castillo in 1897. Cánovas's demise was in retaliation for the imprisonment and torture in Barcelona of many anarchists, anticlerical activists and other less easily classifiable persons also suspected of plotting rebellion. A later victim of the government's antianarchistic policy was Francisco Ferrer, killed in 1909 after he had founded the *Escuela Moderna* in Barcelona, an institution that specialized in antireligious instruction. The sporadic uprisings in Spain of that era were a prelude to the culminating violence of the Civil War (1936–39).

Socialism and anarchism starting in the 1890s and—from 1898

on—each of the writers' personalized nonconformity were brewing together with religious uncertainties and a skeptical view of the future. The same heterogeneity referred to by Gullón had become a fundamental characteristic of the generation. Its members' preoccupations and nostalgias, and their new perspectives on the Spanish landscape lent them a feeling of congeniality. Their melancholy— articulated by Azorín in *La voluntad* (1902), Baroja en *El árbol de la ciencia* (1911) and Antonio Machado in *Campos de Castilla* (1912) and complemented by the doleful gazes in Picasso's "blue period" portraits—confirmed the pessimism expressed in a phrase by Cánovas years before: "Spaniards are those unable to be anything else." Federico de Onís reflects metaphorically on his compatriots' inclination toward intellectual isolation by observing: "The Spaniard floats on a different civilization from his own without mixing with it—like oil on water." ("Julio Camba," Onís's introduction to his edition for students of Camba's *La rana viajera* (New York: MacMillan, 1928).

Cánovas may have been right about the Spaniard's "inability" to be anything else. But the will to create finds strange sources of inspiration; the "Disaster" and the sense of futility it expressed operated as a stimulus as well as a paradox. Consider Miguel de Unamuno's declaration in "Mi religión" (the opening essay of *Mi religión y otros ensayos*, 1907–9): "My religion is to seek truth in life and life in truth, with full awareness that I won't find them as long as I live." With the same energetic hopelessness but in an obviously more ironic vein, Azorín (*La voluntad*) presents the inventor Alonso Quijano, of clearly symbolic first and last names, and his weapon of misguided destruction, the *toxpiro*. We're told that Quijano's rickety rocket carries only one kilo, six hundred grams of dynamite, instead of the six hundred kilos recommended by "the technicians," and that seven abortive test flights in one day confirm its total failure. No matter; faulty application is superseded by inventive pride. José Martínez Ruiz ("Azorín"), *La voluntad*, María Martínez del Portal, ed. (Madrid: Ediciones Cátedra, 1997, 180–81). Such is the case also with the surgeon in Julio Camba's *La rana viajera* (1928), who after a few deft but careless strokes of the scalpel, leaves a patient dead on the operating table, claiming with no trace of remorse that his performance was an "artistic success." Julio Camba "El virtuosismo de la cirugia" in *La rana viajera, Obras completas* (Madrid: Editorial Plus-Ultra, 1948) 1: 532–33. For his part, Alonso Quijano believes his fizzled experiment is still a major contribution to military science, and one of the reporters gathered at the test site in Yecla shares his enthusiasm: "Naval warfare will be revolutionized; battleships will be useless. From a launching pad on the coast the *toxpiro* will explode its dynamite against their thick armor and the thick armor will be blown to bits. Spain will be powerful once more; Gibraltar will be ours; great powers will seek our alliance. And the venerable double-faced eagle will again soar majestically over Europe." *La voluntad*, 181.

Fictionalized attitudes toward Spain's military status and the Spanish American War were not much stranger than the real ones. Compare the patriotic ebullience of Azorín's journalist in *La voluntad* with that of Captain General Basilio Augustín (the Spanish officer in charge of defending the Philippines), who in April, 1898, sent this telegram to his superiors in Madrid: "The struggle will be short and decisive. The God of victories will grant us one commensurate with the reason and justice of our cause." (quoted by Federico Bravo Morata in *Fin del siglo y de las colonias*, Madrid: Fenicia, 1972, 174).

Together with Ortega's formula for a generation (what is received combined with what is spontaneous), certain personal traits in common can be appropriately considered. The writers of 1898 were all perceived to be eccentric intellectuals (*raros*) and rugged individualists. Each was from a different region of the country but joined the others—sometimes in Madrid, sometimes by correspondence, sometimes polemically in the form of literary criticism—in a new awareness of Spain as a "problem." Each in his way was a romantic, with a poetic love of landscape, of a past suggestive, in Unamuno's mind, of "eternity," and of quiet small-town life. Each was a cultural and/ or political extremist; in the 1890s Azorín, Unamuno, and Ramiro de Maeztu professed varieties of socialism tinged with anarchy (on this topic see *Juventud del 98* by Carlos Blanco Aguinaga, 1970, and *Política y sociedad en el primer Unamuno* by Rafael Pérez de la Dehesa, 1966) that were too individualistic to materialize in the form of concrete political action.

Baroja, the perpetual iconoclast, disbelieved in social progress and dismissed the hopes that Maeztu expressed in *Hacia otra España* (1899) for the "regeneration" of Spain. In part 4, ch. 4 of *El árbol de la ciencia* (New York: Las Ameicas Publishing Co., n.d.) he declares that humanity will always opt for cruelty or evil, in the spirit of "the Holy Mother's Church that used to cut off the Sistine Chapel's sing-

ers' testicles so they could sound better."[2] In part 2 of *Paradox, rey*
(1906) a modernist cyclops nestled in a dark mountain delivers a
"Metaphysical Praise of Destruction" (chapter 12) that begins: "To
destroy is to change; that's all" and ends: "To destroy is to change.
No, there's more. To destroy is to create." *Paradox, rey* (Jesús Ma.
Lasaga Baster, ed., Madrid: Espasa-Calpe, 1991, p. 170). For Baroja
there's no positive way out; he takes infirmity and bad outcomes for
granted. His medical training was undoubtedly a factor; on its com-
pletion he submitted a fifty-two-page doctoral thesis (*El dolor: estudio
psicofísico)* to the Universidad Central in Madrid. He practiced as a
physician only about two years, but his subsequent literary work elab-
orates on those early diagnostic perceptions. His view of people is
intensely "natural," as a biologist—but also a psychologist—might
see them. In the characters of his novels he diagnoses their temperament, physical, and physiological features, the strength or weakness
of their wills, their signs of hysteria or madness, their nervous tension, etc. Lulú (in *El árbol de la ciencia*) is a sickly young woman whose
condition blends well with her author's glum view of life; Fernando
Ossorio (*Camino de perfección*) suffers from fevers and dizzy spells that
symbolize his artistic and mystic passions; Bizco ("Cross-eyes") in *La
busca* (1904) is a collage of brutality, repugnance and evil intentions—clearly hated as well as despised by Baroja: "*Bizco's* face produced an ugly creature's attraction for the pathologist. His narrow
forehead, Roman nose, thick lips, freckled skin and stiff red hair reminded one of a large, blond baboon. . . . If he came across a stray
cat or dog he'd stab it to death with his knife, taking pleasure in its
martyrdom. He was inarticulate, filling his speech with obscenities
and curses."

The closest personal relationship in the generation, though also
the shortest, was that of Unamuno and Angel Ganivet (1865–98)
who were university classmates in Madrid in the1880s and who
shared in their writings a persistent desire for modern man's spiritual regeneration. Ganivet was—in society, culture, and his own marriage—a solitary misfit. His protagonist in *Los trabajos del infatigable
creador Pío Cid* shares his extreme skepticism: "A man, at his very
best, is worth less than the volume of air that he displaces" *Los trabajos del infatigable creador Pío Cid*, José Montero Padilla, ed. (Madrid:
Clásicos Castalia, 1998), 406–7. He served in the consular service
and spent his last six years abroad. His final act was a suicide leap
into an ice-choked river in Finland in November 1898. Ganivet's

best-known work, *Idearium español* (completed in 1896) seeks a cultural remedy for the average Spaniard's alleged national malady: *abulia*, which meant hopelessness and lack of will. He argues that Spain's strength has always been based on its "spiritual energy" rather than its military or political power. Ultimately, his will to spiritual energy was outweighed by the pessimism that culminated in his suicide.

Each of the generation's members who wrote novels emphasized (or exploited) the role of his protagonist as alter ego in a voice that expressed dissent, spiritual perplexity, or skepticism. Their function was not to create full three-dimensional characters in the nineteenth-century realist tradition, but to express neoromantic moods that reflected their own predilections and phobias. They were impressionists and *pensadores* ("thinkers") who in the spirit of Unamuno and Ganivet asked mostly unanswerable questions. José Ruiz Martínez uses his universally accepted pen name, *Azorín*, for his protagonist in *La voluntad* and in *Antonio Azorín*; and Tomás Rueda, his modern version of Cervantes' Tomás Rodaja in *El licenciado Vidriera*, is more than anything a thinly veiled self-portrait. *Tomás Rueda* (1915), the author tells us in his 1941 prologue to a later edition, is a "novelistic essay" on Cervantes' short work.

Cervantes' protagonist is an adventurer who becomes as the psychosomatic result of a serious illness an acerbic social critic. Crowds gather to hear his opinions; judges, poets, muleteers, and doctors suffer his whiplashes indiscriminately, for all—he says—operate on the basis of corrupt self-interest. He has been poisoned in revenge by a woman who aspired to become his lover and, awaking from the prolonged coma that the poisoning provoked, believes he's made of glass and fears, literally, breaking apart. Cervantes' Tomás Rodaja is transformed into the psychically brittle Licenciado Vidriera. His poisoning has given him new lucidity. He performs volubly, in a state of outgoing agitation, a miniature, Socratic Don Quijote without horse or squire. But when he regains rationality, he loses his acumen; so his listeners diminish, then disappear altogether. The spark is gone.

For his part, Azorín's Tomás Rueda lives much more inwardly, in a kind of meditative ecstasy animated by the slow-moving, small-town world around him. Like his precursor, he has studied and earned his *licenciatura* at Salamanca and has served as a soldier in Flanders and Italy. In a less drastic but equally significant way he's described in the eleventh of the book's thirteen short chapters as "glass-like, a little glass-like." No toxicant is involved. Living has simply become an apprehensive experience. Tomás is now aware of his new edginess, and a more "irritable and sickly" sensibility. His perceptions have sharpened, but at the cost of a nagging uneasiness. Accordingly, he seeks solitude as a possible means of gaining self-determination. Withdrawal from the everyday world is necessary; "a life of communication and steady expansion would have resulted in his failure to be himself." Since—for both Azorín and his inward-gazing protagonist—the future is an unknowable attraction, the story ends, in Flanders, with no end. Tomás has received a letter from an unidentified person "which reads as follows . . .", but none of the text of the letter is revealed. Mysteries, Azorín clearly believes, are more interesting than solutions or "closures."

There could be no greater contrast than that which existed between the generation's subjectivity and touchy temperaments and the preceding realist movement, whose members patiently assembled and utilized everything possible for their narratives.

Benito Pérez Galdós's genius manifested itself in the obsessions, tics, and quirks of his character developments. The Fortunata of his lengthy *Fortunata y Jacinta* (1887) was a unique woman at the same time she was "every" woman. Her actions and thought were candid rejections of the social vanities of her era. In contrast, Doña Paca in *Misericordia* (1897) Rosalía and Francisco de Bringas of *La de Bringas* (1884) appear as symbols of a still-active but moribund culture of retentiveness typical of the 1870s. A tedious emblem of the era is the glued-hair cenotaph described in tedious detail at the beginning of *La de Bringas*. The declining way of life fuzzily consecrated in Don Francisco's creation—"What should we call it?" is the first sentence in the novel—held little or no attraction for the writers of 1898.[3]

Born between 1824 (Juan Valera) and 1853 (Armando Palacio Valdés) and including Emilia Pardo Bazán—who was also a naturalist—and José María de Pereda—the entrenched representative of local color—the realist writers of the late nineteenth century did not constitute a generation.[4] They shared a fascination for the minutiae of a present (fashion, social behavior, customary routines, physical appearance, the importance of objects as well as subjects in the representation of luxury, poverty, and bourgeois norms) that was overburdened with past traditions. They expressed little interest—in contrast to the more apprehensive Generation of 1898—in what the future might bring. They wrote in the perspective of an invisible character functioning as witness. In their quest of objectivity they focused on conditions and circumstances that reflected the scarcely perceptible, involuntary changes taking place during the "Restauración" (1874–1900) of the Spanish monarchy. On the other hand, they were not inclined to protest or dissent, whether individual or organized.

It's important to note that these authors attracted relatively little biographical interest, whereas from the time of their earliest publications Unamuno, Baroja, Machado, and—especially—Valle-Inclán generated innumerable anecdotes, legends, and caricatures. Basically they were loners, yet they lived centrifugally, frequently encountering one another whether in person or in writing. They had the implicit and sometimes explicit collaboration of their alter egos, and created their own legends; they were confessional by nature—not for errant ways that burdened their conscience, but for inner compulsions that needed a literary outlet. For the same reason, their narratives were meditative and often in the spirit of a memoir, and—like Unamuno—Baroja and Azorín were accomplished essayists.

In 1904 Unamuno published an essay, "A lo que salga" that marks an important turning point in his creative process and, at the same time, highlights an essential difference between the earlier realists and the more subjective writers of his own time. In "A lo que salga" he distinguishes between "oviparous" and "viviparous" writing. He had first followed the former (slower) more meticulous process during the 1890s and, notably, in *Paz en la Guerra* (1898), his first novel. But then, he reveals, "recently I began feeling the urge to become a viviparous writer" ("A lo que salga," in *Nuestro Tiempo* [Madrid, Sept. 1904]. The zoological metaphors are most appropriate. Oviparous creation is slow, deliberate, carefully researched or documented where necessary. First the egg is hatched, then the writer "incubates" it as a narrative realist or naturalist would. Viviparous writing, as the word suggests, is the equivalent of live birth. Its practitioners "carry everything in their heads" and when they have their idea, "when their real labor pains start . . . they sit down, take pen in hand, and give birth." Miguel de Unamuno, "A lo que salga" in *Obras completas* (Madrid: Escelicer, 1966, 1:1196). Carried to a further extreme ("a lo que salga": *whatever comes out),* oviparous writing would have been an equivalent—for novels and essays—to the surrealist method ("automatic writing") that in his manifestos of the 1920s André Breton applied to poetry.

The spontaneous penchant evident in many of the eccentric characters (Azorín's Alonso Quijano, Valle-Inclán's Marqués de Bradomín, and Máximo Estrella—the protagonist of *Luces de Bohemia* (1924) based on Alejandro Sawa, a bohemian journalist and frequenter of the generation's tertulias in Madrid—Baroja's neo-Hegelian Professor Werden, Unamuno's rebellious Augusto Pérez) is a reflection of their authors' often volatile temperaments. In *Días y caminos de España* (1997) the Argentine writer Rubén Benítez recalls that Pío Baroja never forgave Valle-Inclán the swift kick allegedly inflicted on Baroja's friendly dog during Valle's first and probably last visit to Baroja's home. Unamuno also had his outbursts—including those contained in personal letters referring to the dictator Miguel Primo de Rivera's role in exiling him from Spain in 1924, and his spontaneous reaction against the Nationalist General Millán Astray's notorious cry ("Death to Intelligence!") during a public ceremony at the University of Salamanca on October 12, 1936 that resulted (the next day) in Unamuno's dismissal as Rector of the University. But Unamuno's temperament—in contrast to Valle-Inclán's more aesthetically motivated gut reactions (for him, kicking the dog in Baroja's house was a form of aesthetic expression as much as a gesture of repulsion)—is basically ideological and spiritual, as is clearly evident in the emphasis throughout his works on religion-complicated-by-doubt, existential anxiety, and quixotic idealism.

Closely linked to these vivid and often conflictive relationships among the generation's members, and between its members and the authorities, was the recurrent confrontation of two cultural perceptions: the Spanish one, and the one that Unamuno and Ortega y Gasset saw as "European" or "Europeanized." In March, 1908 Ortega had set forth in a letter to Don Miguel opinions that amounted to an anti-Unamuno manifesto: "The love of science, clarity and order is what unites us in brotherhood. Let's swear that as of today the secular Spanish sin, the sin against the Holy Spirit, the hatred of science, is ended. Suppose the results of science are only transitory. Suppose those of mysticism are more comfortable. So what? Science doesn't consist of results, but of method: the method of spiritual rectitude, the virtue of masculine veracity as opposed to feminine sincerity." The letter is reproduced in Laureano Robles and Antonio

Ramos Gascón, eds., *Epistolario completo Ortega-Unamuno* (Madrid: Ediciones El Arquero, 1987), 78–79.

Still more blunt was a previous and longer letter that Ortega wrote to Unamuno from the University of Marburg in Germany (December 30, 1906) when the author was only twenty-three. There he strongly insinuated, albeit in the friendliest terms, that more than anyone else the Rector of the University of Salamanca was guilty of "frantic mysticism," (see Robles and Ramos Gascón, *Epistdaría completa*, 55–61) which Ortega considered a generational vice (of the Generation of 1898, that is), and the latest symptom of Spain's long-evolving intellectual exclusion from Europe.

Clothed in appropriate insults, the rationalist versus mysticist polemic raged on, and it's no exaggeration to say that Ortega y Gasset, "excessively Germanized" in the opinion of Unamuno, left indelible marks on the generation's thought in general and—in partcular—on Unamuno's masterwork *Del sentimiento trágico la vida en los hombres y en los pueblos* (1913), in the first chapter of which ("El hombre de carne y hueso") he pointedly remarks: "Indeed, there are persons who seem to think using the brain alone, or any other organ specifically needed to think; while others think with their whole body and soul, with their blood, marrow and bones, with their heart and lungs, with their lives" (*Obras completas* 7:117) [see p. 175] and: "If a philosopher is not a man, he's anything but a philosopher; he is, above all, a pedant, the mockery of a man" (p. 118).

Ortega always took a skeptical view of the Hispanic tradition and, generally, of the temperament's role in literary or philosophical thought. He obviously opposed Unamuno's role as the Generation of 1898's spiritual leader, and for reasons of age, historical perspective, and differences in ideology could never have been one of the generation's participants. Yet, for those same reasons and the acuity of his criticism, he performed a vital role in the generation's development. In effect, his whiplashes repeatedly spurred Unamuno on to greater intensity in his thinking and writing.

Adequate definition and evaluation of a generation requires taking into account their shared experiences, and their perspectives—both individual and collective—on historical change. Between 1891, when Unamuno was awarded the departmental chair of Greek Language and Literature at the University of Salamanca, and 1924, when he was dismissed as Rector by order of Primo de Rivera, Antonio Machado, Azorín, Valle-Inclán, Unamuno, and Baroja all produced their most important works. But the influence of those writers was to continue long after.

Clearly, the generation's most active vital phase began in the spring of 1898 with the conflict called "the Disaster" by its losers and "the Splendid Little War" by its victors, and continued until 1936, when Spain experienced the cataclysm of General Franco's nationalist rebellion. The intellectual atmosphere was first incited (in 1898) and ultimately desolated (between 1936 and 1939) by the disillusionment that war and political crisis inevitably bring.

The civil war that broke out in July 1936 definitively marks the end of the Generation's era. In that year Unamuno, Valle-Inclán, and Maeztu died (like Federico García Lorca, Maeztu was killed by one of the civil war's opposing factions). And that year Antonio Machado's *Juan de Mairena*, first published serially in *Diario de Madrid* and *El Sol*, came out in book form. This miscellany can be read as an informal postscript to the generation's work. Like Ganivet's, Unamuno's, Azorín's, Baroja's, and Valle-Inclán's autobiographically imbued narratives, *Juan de Mairena* is written in the perspective of the author's alter ego, the "declarations, witticisms, notes, and recollections of an apocryphal professor," as the subtitle reads. In most of its fifty chapters Juan de Mairena lectures his students, frequently referring to philosophers, poets and artists of other times, as well as to his mentor and former professor, Abel Martín, whom he often quotes. The intellectual team of Machado and his fictional colleagues Mairena and Martín share the spirit of Unamuno's *Del sentimiento trágico* in expressing their creative skepticism: "Great poets are failed metaphysicians." "Great philosophers are poets who believe in the reality of their poems" (22). They would like to replace restrictive religion with a practical variety of wisdom in the Platonic tradition, and in chapter 35 Mairena proposes the foundation of a "Popular Institute of Superior Wisdom" that would be instrumental in stimulating its students to think more and believe less.

Between 1898 and 1936, other situations, events, appearances and disappearances affected the Generation's outlook. Angel Ganivet's previously mentioned suicide (1898); Rubén Darío's arrival in Madrid from Buenos Aires as correspondent for *La Nación* (January 1899); the death of Leopoldo Alas (*Clarín*), the prestigious—and mordacious—critic of the new writers, especially Unamuno and Darío (1902); the petition (1905) signed by Azorín, Unamuno, Darío, Maeztu, Valle-Inclán, Baroja, and others denouncing the

award of the Nobel Prize to old-fashioned Spanish playwright José
Echegaray in 1904; the assassination in Barcelona of Francisco Ferrer, the anarchist leader (1909); the death of Marcelino Menéndez
Pelayo, conservative literary historian and defender of the traditions
negatively scrutinized by most of the Generation (1910); the general
strike in Spain (1917) alluded to in Valle Inclán's *Luces de Bohemia*
by the blind poet-protagonist Max Estrella who in scene 4 declares
"My heart is with the people"; General Primo de Rivera's coup
d'état (1923) which led to Unamuno's exile the following year; a
new, but basically weak republic (1931); and finally, sporadic labor
unrest and revolutionary ferment over the five years preceding the
Civil War. In sum, Spanish civilization was viewed in the dim light of
dying traditions and faltering institutions.

In conclusion two general attitudes can be considered as basic elements of the Generation of 1898. One is their consistent combining,
almost in the form of a new genre, of philosophical thought and a
poetic spirit in what they wrote. Not only are the generation's works
more lyrical and meditative than those of their predecessors; they
also show an obsession with history as a metaphor of paradox and
confusion. The obsession is as strong in the essay as in poetry and
fiction. The generation's writers were voracious readers of modern
philosophy: Hegel, Kant, Schopenhauer, Kierkegaard, Nietzsche,
William James, and, before them, Spinoza (on the importance of
Nietzsche see Gonzalo Sobejano's book *Nietzsche en España*, 1967).
They were less interested in those philosophers' ideological systems
than in their implicit meditative experiences—for example: Azorín's
reiterations on the theme of eternal return adapted from Nietzsche;
and Unamuno's fascination with the will to believe gleaned from his
reading of James.

The second attitude is evident in the writers' overwhelming subjectivity that consistently leads to existential uncertainty. Storytelling
for them was not a bipolar relationship of author and character, but
rather a dynamic projection of the writer in his tripartite relationship of *author-character-actor*. In addition to their alter egos, Baroja,
Unamuno, Machado, Valle-Inclán, and Azorín give us a metaphorical landscape that is precarious and impressionistic. Its storms and
calms appear to be directed by the authors' moods.

A skeptical foreboding prevails in their evaluations: the quixotic
Alonso Quijano's *toxpiro* described by Azorín follows the path of
Spain's resistance to invasion in Cuba and the Philippines; it has to

flop. Baroja's Professor Werden in *La caverna del humorismo* (1919) finds only one escape route from the human experience of deformity, injustice, and corruption. All these faults, he happily concludes, "ensure the existence of *humorism*" (my emphasis) which is the sweet-and-sour sauce of Spanish life. Philosophical uncertainty, which was the staple of the generation's edginess, is particularly evident in *Juan de Mairena*. In that work uncertainty—but uncertainty clearly seen—is the recurrent stimulus for Abel Martín, author, it should be recalled, of a eighteen-hundred-page opus, *Sobre la esencial heterogeneidad del ser*. More than once a developing uncertainty reaches the extreme of absurdity. In chapter 31 the tripartite author (Machado assisted by Martín and Mairena) sets forth the paradox that "something that is" can suddenly throw us into the realization that "this same something is not" (i.e., doesn't exist or is really something else). This is the idea, whether taken to be judicious or absurd, behind Abel Martín's concept of *otredad* or *alteridad trascendente* (33).

Curiously—and usually with no recognition of Antonio Machado, its prestigious inventor—the concept was to acquire a vogue of epidemic proportions among academic literary theorists of the late twentieth century. *Otherness* and *alterity* are words that pepper the pages of scholarly books and articles, in which the authors' purposes are as varied as metaphysical exploration in the creative mind, gender theory in literature, and optional or alternative "lifestyles" in contemporary life.

Unamuno, the poet-thinker of "*esto y aquello*," also develops a concept of continuous susceptibility to otherness: especially in the closing pages of *Niebla* (1914), where the invasive nothingness that afflicts both the book's author and its protagonist is described. With Don Quijote and his own Augusto Pérez in mind, Unamuno has invented the words *nivola* and *nivolesco* to indicate a third, intermediate status between fact and imaginative creation. Augusto knows that physical existence (in particular, that of Cervantes or Unamuno) is perishable and time-restricted, and that the imagined existence of fictional characters is immortal and free and, further, that the fictional character's freedom is something to be shared by generations of readers to come. At the end of chapter 31, Augusto ascribes to his author the same ambivalent or *nivolesco* status that he has suffered as his protagonist: "you're just one more *nivolesque* entity, like your *nivolesque* readers, and like me, Augusto Pérez your victim" (*Obras completas* 2: p. 670).

The Generation of 1898 lived, read and wrote with a sense of historical insecurity and foreboding. They were vital thinkers and should judged primarily in that light. Their call for cultural regeneration was loud and clear. In different yet beneficial ways, Ortega y Gasset (the generation's uppity stepson?), Juan Ramón Jiménez ("*a la minoría, siempre*"), the poets of another generation—that of 1927—and Camilo José Cela (inheritor of Baroja's grim skepticism) assimilated their energy and their light. Its members' gestures, subjective portraits, and panoramas are as alive today as they were a century ago.

9

In and Out of Time: Cervantes, Dostoevsky, Borges, García Márquez

> Time travels in divers paces with
> divers persons.
>
> —Shakespeare

DURING A TELEVISION INTERVIEW I WATCHED IN SANTIAGO IN SEPTEMBER 1995, General Augusto Pinochet was asked what—six years after the end of his rule—he thought Chile needed the most. His answer in four slowly enunciated syllables could not have been more emphatic: "*El ol-vi-do*," forget it all. Oblivion was his prescription for Chileans and foreigners alike, the simplest way to whitewash a military regime's past crimes. Within the mold of García Márquez's composite dictator portrayed in *El otoño del patriarca* (1975), Pinochet in uneasy retirement was still following an elementary procedure of dictatorship: the quiet elimination of incriminating evidence.[1] In a broader sense the general was demonstrating—unintentionally, of course—that authoritarian power works to make us forget the same scenes and situations that eyewitness testimonies and literary recollection help us remember.

Mario Vargas Llosa once observed that literature—especially in its narrative forms—has been the most reliable source for judging reality in Latin America. By contrast, the frequently biased or censored news media and a variety of self-serving witnesses have traditionally obfuscated the truth. To be sure, in Latin America literature readers have an opportunity to experience the continuous tension between those who try to cancel out or truncate reality under the guise of forgetfulness, and those who aspire to reconstruct the essential elements of reality in the form of art. *Cien años de soledad* (1967) and Isabel Allende's *La casa de los espíritus* (1982) are lucid examples of

134

how the tension between concealment and revelation should be handled in flexible frameworks of historical and personal time. Yet, these narrators, like Tomás Eloy Martínez in the political caprices and phantasmal endurance of his celebrity-protagonist in *Santa Evita* (1995), skillfully adapt the propensities and wily deceptions of unliterary others to their satirical performances.

In her thoughts on the uses of time in fiction, Eudora Welty finds its "deepest meaning" in our mortality.[2] Indisputably, the four writers discussed in this chapter lived and wrote "in mortal light," in experiences they intimately shared with their protagonists and all the secondary characters who interacted with them. Mortality—as is clearly seen in a short story of Welty's I comment on in chapter 6 ("A Worn Path")—is the most compelling and paradoxically the most "vital" measurement in literature. Mortality, figuratively and literally, imposes itself as the main preoccupation of our lives. It affects the author's and his or her characters' caprices and aspirations, sets the pace of their activity, delineates their imagination of the future, and more.

The elusive yet ever-present Melquíades—who functions as García Márquez's spectral coauthor—had written in an epigraph to his prophetic parchments an exact account of what Aureliano discovers as the novel ends. In that epigraph he finds, *while it is happening,* that his newborn son, the Buendías's last representative (a "swollen, dried-out lump of flesh"), is being dragged off by ants to be consumed by them. Aureliano also reads in the parchments that he'll die in a windstorm together with all the rest of Macondo's inhabitants as soon as he gets to the last page. Like the first member of the Buendía clan, the little victim of nibbling ants was also born with a pigtail. And the reiterated pigtail symbolizes with comic pessimism the predetermined extinction of an aimless, intermarrying family, of Macondo and—by extension—of a whole nation's potential for progress and harmony. The family's fate is a microcosm of history. In the climax of *Cien años de soledad*, past and present merge, as Octavio Paz would express it, in a "perpetual present."

At the end, as in many of his preceding experiences, Aureliano Buendía senses that he has been living simultaneously in past and present. Macondo amid its marshlands and its proximity to the sea was a historical kaleidoscope in which the image of Sir Francis Drake, who for his amusement allegedly fired cannonballs at crocodiles on the shore from one of his galleons, coincides with an unnamed banana company's exploitations (clearly, those of the United Fruit Co.) in the 1920s.[3] Macondo's founder José Arcadio Buendía had envisioned it as a happy community as well as a station on the uncertain route, northward of course, to "civilization."

In Macondo, as in Don Quijote's landscapes and Borges's hallucinating scenarios, time imposes itself as the characters struggle to elude it. The mysteries of clock, calendar, heritage, and future await the reader on the most revealing pages of *Don Quijote*, for example: in the Cave of Montesinos episode and in the Duke's and Duchess's palace; in the amnesia epidemic and the extendible existences of people and things in *Cien años de soledad*; in Dostoevsky's disturbing perceptions of death-in-life in several of his novels; in H. G. Wells's *The Time Machine*, a fantasy in which the time-traveller describes his view of the world in the year 802,701 A.D.

Life, in mortal light, acquires a new sharpness of vision. Early in part 1 of *The Idiot* (1868) Prince Lev Nikolayevich Myshkin comments on the intensity and fullness of time experienced by a condemned man in Lyon who's scheduled to die by the guillotine a few minutes later. Consider also Jorge Luis Borges's "El milagro secreto," for that story (in characteristically circuitous detail) the author creates a protagonist who by circumstance parallels the figure recalled by Prince Myshkin. Jaromir Hladik, a Jewish writer in Prague, is arrested in his apartment by the German Gestapo on March 19, 1939 and imprisoned.[4] Ten days later he'll be executed by a firing squad. In Hladik's last moments author and reader are privy to his thoughts. Was Borges, inadvertently or by design, taking up where Dostoevsky left off? Whether or not he had the Russian's text in mind, he clearly shared his curiosity over the mental effects of imminent death and found just the imaginary event he needed as a literary counteraction to one of the terrifying realities of Nazi power before and during World War II. With Borges's timely encouragement, God grants Hladik's special request: a full year's writing time to complete his unfinished play, *Los enemigos*, before the fusillade that will wipe him out within two minutes of that psychologically agitated yet intellectually serene prayer.

Unique as it was, Hladik's experience had important antecedents. Two of them are executions referred to in *The Idiot*. As is well known, Fyodor Dostoevsky—prosecuted as a political dissident at the age of twenty-eight—was escorted on December 22, 1849 to a scaffold in St. Petersburg for his own execution. But the sentence was commuted just before the appointed moment and later reduced to four years in a Siberian prison. So the author knew from personal experience what he and Prince Myshkin were talking about. Myshkin's reference to the execution in Lyon reflects Dostoevsky's commitment to social justice. His fascination with individual human obsessions and depravities didn't deter him from denouncing institutionalized capital punishment as the worst of crimes. The prince declares, "To kill for murder is an immeasurably greater evil than the crime itself. Judicial murder is immeasurably more horrible than one committed by a robber."

But judicial murder is also appropriate food for narrative thought—as is dynamically clear in four of the best known Hispanic-American dictator novels: García Márquez's *El otoño del patriarca*, Carpentier's *El recurso del método*, Asturias's *El señor Presidente*, and Vargas Llosa's *La fiesta del chivo*. Further on in *The Idiot* Dostoevsky tells of a case in which a Borgesian kind of motif is clearly discernible. With Jaromir Hladik's postponed death in mind, we hear Myshkin again during his first visit with the Yepanchin family.

The episode he recalls this time—of a twenty-seven-year-old prisoner who is reprieved minutes before his scheduled execution—is the author's reliving of his own traumatic experience (and at the same age: twenty-seven) in St. Petersburg. Myshkin's "acquaintance," whom he has met in Switzerland), recalls that the last five minutes "seemed to him an eternity, an immense richness." Of those last five minutes he would allot two to saying goodbye to his fellow prisoners, two more "to reflect on himself," and with what was left "to look about him for the last time." The final reflecting and looking around entail a strange existential awareness; ultimately the condemned man "would merely be *something*—something or somebody, but who, though? And where?" His quandary is intensified at that point by the sun's gleam on the gilded roof of a church close by. "He couldn't drag his eyes away: it occurred to him that those rays were his new state of being, and that in three minutes he would somehow merge with them."[5] The sunlight has given him his image of eternity.

Still, there's a notable difference between Hladlik's emotions and those of Dostoevsky's figure, which can be taken as a clear reflection of their authors' personalities and concerns. Whereas the condemned man in *The Idiot* reacts temperamentally against the judicial process, Borges's protagonist surmounts his own dread creatively. In contrast to Hladik's role as intellectual winner and his consequent gratitude for a miniscule lease on life, Myshkin's friend's reaction as the unequivocal loser is one of rage and resentment. With so little time left he's overwhelmed by the clash between his desire for survival and the certainty of his extinction. "What if I didn't have to die! If life were returned to me what an eternity it would be! And it would be all mine! I would turn every minute into an age."[6] The condensed-or-expanded time phenomenon, of course, wasn't new. It had figured prominently, among other places, in the Cueva de Montesinos episode in part 2 of *Don Quijote*. On emerging from the cave the Don asks his squire how long he was down there and Sancho Panza answers "a little over an hour" (chapter 23). In that adventure, as well as in *The Idiot* and "El milagro secreto," contradictory times are in play. Had a little over an hour passed, as Sancho said? Or had the explorer remained in the mysterious place, as he steadfastly claimed, three days and nights? No decision is necessary. In the two characters' fictional realm neither testimony need be denied. Each experience had been *lived* as it was described. The author was fully aware that physical and mental times don't necessarily coincide, that our intervals in a waking state or in a dream—though often mixed in our recollections—can also function independently of one another.

Cervantes' art, of which there are magical echoes in Borges and García Márquez, was vibrantly visual: not in celebrations of color, texture, or landscape, nor in a precision of portraiture (such as in the works of Pérez Galdós or Alejo Carpentier), but in the kinds of gesture and perception—often presented in dialogue—that intensify unexpected visions and often capitalize on invasions of the *real* by the *unreal.* It was visual in what could be called a choreography of situations. Dulcinea and the same two country girls with whom Don Quijote saw her before (in part 2, chapter 10) execute *cabriolas* across the dream stage of Montesinos. Near the beginning (1:8) Don Quijote tangles spectacularly with one of the giants disguised as windmills. Much later (2:41) a magic voyage is staged (literally) in the Duke and Duchess's palace. The circumstances of that real world in real time are displaced with the aid of a blindfold and a wooden horse. With Sancho seated behind him on Clavileño, Quijote rises swiftly into virtual space, following the virtual route of Icarus, and his squire has no doubt that they've reached the upper "region of fire" simulated by a crew of stage technicians with burning tufts (*estopas*) suspended on poles near the virtual travelers' faces.

As for the Cave of Montesinos, several questions emerge: not only does the reader wonder how long Don Quijote was there, but how he could see as much as he did, how extensive a space it was, what and whom he found (or thought or dreamed he found) and—beyond that—how much longer the knight's continuing will to believe in a lost, multifaceted world of fantasy can contend through most of part 2 with the steadily emerging evidence of its nonexistence. With his chivalric compulsions and imaginative powers, Don Quijote is seldom credited with a recognition of the need to plan ahead, but on this occasion he has the foresight to obtain a hundred fathoms of rope, which as a precaution will be tied to his waist for the descent. The rope's long length, from the start, adds mystery to the cave adventure, an effect comically diminished on Quijote's trip back up, when his weight is felt only as the last twenty fathoms are being hauled in. Cervantes is subtly showing us, with what seems to be merely a casual measurement, that the Don's subterranean wonderland is psychologically closer to reality up on the surface than one would expect. In the first place, the protagonist has relived, in his subterranean dream-state, vitally important past experiences. Secondly, it should be recalled that the excited adventurer has an energetic collaborator on the Montesinos project. The guide who has led him and Sancho to the cave site identifies himself as a *humanista* and researcher (he's a cousin of the university student who appears previously: 2:19). Further, the guide ("*el primo*") is writing a book, *Transformaciones*.[7] The title, it turns out, is most appropriate in the context of the cave exploration to follow. The conscientious guide recommends alertness and urges Quijote to examine "with a hundred eyes everything you see there," and as the knight undertakes his hallucinated exploration there will be plenty for the hundred eyes to take in.

But before he could enjoy the anticipated sights, the Don later recalls, he fell into a deep sleep and awoke (or thought he awoke) on a meadow that surpassed in beauty anything that nature or the imagination could have created. He rubbed his eyes and pinched himself to make sure he was actually who and where he seemed to be. Before him was "a magnificent royal palace or fortress, and its ramparts and walls gleamed like clear crystal," from which old Montesinos himself emerged and invited him in.[8]

The imagination, I noted at the outset, expands, manipulates, or diminishes time at will. Especially when it works within the flexible dimensions of a dream. That is, in the time-and-space scramble that dreams set in motion the imagination is freer to reconstruct events and make unlikely or incongruous things seem plausible than it is in a conscious state of operation.[9] Thus an emblem and flower of knighthood long gone—Montesinos's distinguished cousin and close friend Durandarte—is dramatically present in the great dream-palace within a small, real dream-cave, decorously laid out on a sepulcher. And his figure is not of marble, granite or bronze, "but of real flesh and real bones." Moreover, since he's lying there in *enchanted* form, Durandarte has no need to eat, or to relieve himself of "escrementos mayores." Neither does he have to sleep, and he can listen and talk. Life enhanced by death? Death transformed by life? It makes little difference: literary enchantment has given Durandarte the best of both worlds.

In their separate circumstances both Don Quijote and Prince Myshkin are enchanters, or would-be enchanters, in their compulsion to reshape reality. Myshkin perceives life sporadically, as in a series of trances, the way he wants it to be. Thus at the memorable soirée near the end of part 1, he finds in the sin-encumbered Nastasya a Dulcinea of his own: "In you everything is perfection," he declares. Don Quijote and the prince are also subjected to frequent and diverse disappointments, and each is progressively destroyed by a singular disability to cope with the un-ideal conditions of his contemporary world. To put it another way, each persists in living his own (impossible) time within another (inevitable) time. In a circumstantial and psychological context, of course, Lev Nikolayavich Myshkin and the Knight of the Sorrowful Countenance have much less in common. The former is generally docile and often childlike in demeanor. Deep down, he senses that he can't set things right in a world he sees (tragically) as unacceptable, and young women like the volatile Nastasya Filippovna, a rich man's ex-mistress, and the more impressionable and candid Aglaya Yepanchin are strongly attracted to him. By contrast, Don Quijote confronts (comically) everything he believes is unjust or evil; he flaunts his chivalric book learning and seeks out trouble with exuberant self-confidence, and he appeals to no woman as a possible husband, confidant, or lover.

Nevertheless, as Alan Trueblood points out in a lucid essay, "Dostoevski and Cervantes," several characters in in *The Idiot* find a spiritual bond between the prince and Don Quijote.[10] In the first chapter of part 2 Dostoevsky has Aglaya Yepuchin leave (inadvertently) a love note from the prince in one of her books. When she realizes a week later that the book is *Don Quijote*, she bursts out laughing "for no apparent reason." Called "the poor knight" by Kolya and some other characters further on, the prince is repeatedly shown as vulnerable to the selfish or devious intentions of others, especially those of Parfion Rogozhin, his satanic moral countertype and Nastaya's eventual murderer. Both Myshkin and Don Quijote incite in their observers a mixture of ridicule and compassion. George Steiner reminds us that the prince is "a composite figure with borrowings from Cervantes, Pushkin, and Dickens. His meekness, his unworldly wisdom, his immaculateness of heart—all of which are traits of the implicit Christ, are conveyed in the course of action." These qualities—albeit in the comic dimension that Dostoevsky saw Don Quijote and in the tragically flawed, yet Christ-like, role that his own protagonist was destined to play—are also what give each character his aura of a timeless being. Having almost finished *The Idiot* in early 1868, the author wrote to his niece that in Myshkin he wanted "to depict the positively good man," and "of all the good figures in Christian literature, Don Quixote is the most complete."[11] The underlying paradox that unites Quijote and Myshkin could be called a spiritual oxymoron. That is, each of them is, or senses he is, a timeless being forced—like Christ, both as Savior and Martyr—to live in a finite, contentious, time-infested world.

One of Borges's predestined tasks may have been a creative reduction of Dostoevsky's antiepic gloom. While the Russian seems driven to existential desperation in his life-and-death thoughts and the temperamental performances of several of his characters, Borges finds (with the assistance of the idealist philosophers he reads) a strange stoic and aesthetic consolation when faced with the same problems. The author of *El aleph* (1949) and *Ficciones* (1944) addresses us from a vantage point in his perpetual present; he's the master manipulator of Time in a variety of abstract settings.

Throughout his stories and essays Borges works within a kind of intellectual immunity from the rougher social elements of life that Cervantes, Dostoevsky, and García Márquez continually find themselves exposed to and, consequently, use to literary advantage: the picaresque, political greed, and other corruptions. That immunity helps him reach—in aesthetic and philosophical ways—spectacularly unreal yet persuasive conclusions. Accordingly, in two meticulous, mathematically enhanced pieces that appear in *Discusión* (1932), "Avatares de la tortuga" and "La perpetua carrera de Aquiles y la tortuga," a rabbit-like Achilles—even though he runs ten times faster than the tortoise can waddle—fails to win a handicap race between them. More precisely, the author makes it theoretically impossible for the race to end. In both essays he utilizes Zeno of Elea's "Second Paradox" of infinity: "Achilles runs ten times faster than the tortoise, so he gives him a head-start of ten meters. Thus, while Achilles runs those ten meters, the tortoise walks one. Then, as Achilles runs his next meter, the tortoise ekes out a decimeter, after which Achilles moves a decimeter, barely contested by the tortoise's centimeter, and so on, *ad infinitum.* The result, then, is that there can be no result; the slowing-down process is unalterably progressive, and the end—the moment of the end—is perpetually postponed.

Borges's time-suspension pattern is not limited to those two evocations of Zeno's paradox. He follows it in the unfinished dénouement of "El sur": "Dahlmann firmly grasps the dagger which he may not be able to handle and walks out onto the plain" and, as we have seen, in the one-year writing permission devised for "El milagro secreto."[12] It also prevails in "Las ruinas circulares," in the on-going dream of "another," unseen character who in the last sentence of the story is found to be directing the narrator's existence and fate.

Just as time is readily expendable, in several stories it is subjected to division or multiplication, or to strange convergences in the characters' experiences or situations. In "El sur," when Juan Dahlmann takes his real or virtual train trip (we're deliberately not told whether it's real or dreamed) south to a lonely place on the pampa, and the *almacén* or country tavern where he's confronted by one of the rowdy gauchos, Borges suggests to the reader that the *essential* Juan Dahlmann—a hybrid of the timid, cosmopolitan reader of *A Thousand and One Nights* and the involuntary knife-fighter—is the one who accepts his fate as certain victim in the imminent duel with his offender. The essential Juan Dahlmann, of course, is literally and figuratively a dreamer, strapped to an operating table in Buenos Aires, who thinks (in the imperfect subjunctive: "*hubiera sido*") "it would have been a deliverance, a blessing and a celebration" to die heroically in the time and style of the legendary Martín Fierro. As in "El milagro secreto," Borges has placed his protagonist simultaneously in two contrasting scenarios: Dahlmann in the Buenos Aires clinic about to be anesthetized, and Juan Dahlmann stepping out on the pampa with a borrowed dagger to face his aggressor. The two options intensify the reader's curiosity. "Closure," or *how* the story ends (as in Hemingway's "The Killers") is clearly insinuated, yet the impending duel may simply have been dreamed in the clinic during the fever in which "eight days passed at the pace of eight centuries." The story's main attribute is the artistic and psychological force concentrated in its tragic presentiment, which in turn is conveyed and intensified by an indefinite postponement of the end.

Enamored as he is of metaphysical hypotheses, the author of *Ficciones* further exploits time's potentialities in "El jardín de los senderos que se bifurcan" and "Tlön, Uqbar. Orbis Tertius." In the former Ts'ui Pen is the author of a mysterious manuscript—"un libro y un laberinto" that are one and the same. As explained by the Sinologist Stephan Albert to Ts'ui Pen's great-grandson, the manuscript entitled *El jardín de los senderos que se bifurcan* is a "chaotic novel." Not only is time its central theme; the work also activates Ts'ui Pen's image, "incomplete but not false," of the universe. It's one of Borges's metaphors for a concept of multiple times, including all the "possible ones"—just as the library in "La biblioteca de Babel" contains on its shelves all books to be written in the future as well as those already written. Ts'ui Pen believed, we recall, "in infinite series of times, in a swelling, precarious network of diverging, converging and parallel times."

"Tlön, Uqbar, Orbis Tertius" is Borges's maximum example of time-manipulation and has little need of explanation. The story is based on the assumption that a temporal planet (that is, not spatial or physical) can acquire existence through the will and imagination of a secret society of experts in the arts and sciences, directed in turn by "an obscure individual of genius." There's an insinuation that the secret society owes gratitude to George Berkeley. And in the year (1941) of the story's appearance Berkeley may have twisted immaterially in his grave as Borges carried the philosopher's idealism to the extreme of saying that on Tlön everything is temporal and, (like language) successive; nothing occupies a physical space. The planet's languages have no nouns, and its objects exist exclusively as each individual's visible and audible experiences. Further, those objects can be called forth and disposed of at will; they're "*the poetic necessities*" [my emphasis] that the individual requires.

As with the phantasmal inhabitants of the secret society's invented planet, "poetic necessities" are also the main determinant in Cervantes', Dostoevsky's, Borges's, and García Márquez's *divertimentos* and exasperations with time.

For Cervantes and his figurative stepson ("although I'm like his father, I'm actually Don Quijote's step-father," he tells us in the prologue) time is something dreamed as adventures that are also explorations. Were the descent (inward) into the Cave of Montesinos and the incense-laden virtual flight in the Duke's and Duchess's Palace intended as a gentle parody of the expeditions (outward) and colonial operations in the New World—a region possibly alluded to also in the chapters on Sancho Panza's governorship of the *ínsula Barataria*—a colony questionably granted and questionably administered for what Cervantes considers a bargain price: *barato*? Or is Sancho's tenure as governor of just ten days—as he seems to suggest in his letter to Don Quijote (a subtle allusion to Hernán Cortés's *Cartas de Relación*?)—another opportunity for Cervantes to criticize small-town corruption in peninsular Spain itself?[13]

The four writers dealt with in this chapter appear to have had time concepts that illuminate a shared intuition—mainly psychological, but also intellectual and historical—that led their protagonists toward an ultimate stasis or inertia, as if to suggest that their abandonment in a fictional no-man's-land was historically predetermined.

Borges's figures are left (like Julio Cortázar's Horacio Oliveira precariously poised on an upstairs windowsill at the end of *Rayuela*), arrested in their final tableaux: Hladik stands before the firing squad whose bullets are already in flight; Dahlmann awkwardly grasps his dagger before the imminent duel; in the poetaster Carlos Argentino's basement the true poet of "El aleph" has a *simultaneous* vision (i.e., free of time) of the universe that can be described only in *successive* language (i.e., dominated by time); and in their theoretic foot race the tortoise and Achilles move slower and slower toward a theoretic standstill.

For Dostoevsky the prevailing view is pathological. The "poor knight" in *The Idiot* drifts hopelessly toward his final immobilization. His young life has the aura of a timeless existence enclosing a series of emotional dilemmas. The author portrays Russian society of his time as a convergence of fatefully outspoken, self-destructive individuals, subject in their dialogues and stage-like social encounters to

choleric accesses. What first appear to be momentary whims or caprices are really symptoms of deep obsessions. Temperament deter-
mines behavior. In part 4, when Gavrila Ardalianovich Ivolgin
(Ganya) declares his love to Aglaya she demands that he prove it by
holding his finger to a candle flame. As Prince Myshkin waits ner-
vously in church for the wedding ceremony to begin, his fiancée
Nastaasya Filippovna catches the aristcrat Rogozin's eye in the crowd
outside and shouts "Save me! Take me away! Wherever you like—
now!" This is the same woman who as the volatile hostess of a soirée
in Part I had placed Rogozhin's intended engagement gift, a stack
of one hundred thousand rubles (prosaically wrapped in a copy of
The Stock Exchange News) in the fireplace and, as it began to burn,
promised to marry the first man to retrieve it. The culminating act,
of course, will be Rogozhin's murder of Nastasya (with a knife): a
few hours after rescuing her, the savior will be her killer. On his discovery of the cadaver, with the glaring-eyed Rogozhin as his guide,
Myshkin enters his final phase of helplessness and no longer recog-
nizes the people around him. The same perceptive and sensitive
"poor knight" who has seen so lucidly through the blustering pretensions of his contemporaries ends up as the consummate idiot,
Don Quijote in reverse, with no chance of recovering his sanity.

In his frequent time expansions García Márquez shows a love of
numbers—always hyperbolic and usually specified, like the rain-
storm that lasted "four years, eleven months and two days"—and
superannuation. Within those expansions his personifications range
from the decrepit human-angel hybrid of unknown age or origin in
the brief story "Un hombre muy viejo con unas alas enormes"
(1968) to the protagonist of *El otoño del patriarca* said to have celebrated one August 12 "the first centennial of his rise to power" Gabriel García Márquez, *El otoño del Patriarca* (Barcelona: Plaza & Janés,
1975), p. 216. and long before that to have watched from his window
the arrival of Christopher Columbus's caravels. In between comes
the relatively youthful matriarch of "Los funerales de la Mama
Grande" (1962) who expires after ninety-two years in firmly corrupt
power and whose last utterance—a burp—serves as an amusing fore-
taste to the patriarch's fatal sneezing attack that ends *El otoño*. Not
to forget the widow of Colonel Aureliano Buendía (who had time to
lose thirty-two revolutionary uprisings and fabricated little fishes of
gold to be melted down, then fabricated again, *ad infinitum*), Ursula,
who outlives several generations and comes to realize that time

doesn't really pass, "but circles around itself." The process of Aure-liano's goldfish was a symbol of that circularity. When Ursula dies she's estimated to have lived between 115 and 122 years.

It should be noted that despite their deep differences in ideology, social background, and motivation, García Márquez and Borges are both fascinated with the idea that what happens now was written be-fore—as the geniuses who designed the time-based planet in "Tlön, Uqbar, Orbis Tertius" and the gypsy Melquíades foresee in *Cien años de soledad*. Further, the two writers feel a common attraction for time viewed as a convergence of *simultaneous* occurrences and *successive* ones, and—with Octavio Paz—an intuition of the Eternal Present.

From Cervantes to García Márquez the process of diminished her-oism—i.e., the hero considered as a tragic figure—is unmistakable. At the same time, the power of irony and ridicule has increased and coincided with a growing self-curiosity that in Borges's and García Márquez's narratives reaches a high degree of fascination. The pre-occupation with self has also bred alter egos, as I've suggested in chapter 8, without resorting to the easier fix of Narcissism. Usually it has brought author and his or her characters psychologically closer together and provoked a sharper, more critical, more comic view of reality. Critical acumen, after all, is the foundation on which good comedy is built. Ortega y Gasset has correctly seen (in *Meditaciones del Quijote*) that comedy has for the most part displaced tragedy in the modern mind. "The transferal of heroic character from *will* to *perception* [my emphasis] has caused the entanglement of tragedy, its disintegration, its comedy."

Perception, whether splendidly clear or absurdly distorted, is what remains, and what impresses us. In the end, Myshkin has been un-ceremoniously returned to the Swiss clinic and left in bed with glazed eyes and mouth open; Juan Dahlmann, unfamiliar dagger in hand, approaches his adversary (or dreams that he approaches him) on a darkened pampa; in Don Quijote's case more of a sense of fi-nality prevails: the hero has died and Sansón Carrasco has written his epitaph. Yet the question persists: are the Knight's return home, his repudiation of magical phenomena and his calm, final self-recognition a spiritual triumph or a poetic loss? Should Unamuno in his *Vida de Don Quijote y Sancho* have used Quijote's death as the ultimate symbol of his immortality? "Death," he writes, "is our im-mortalizer." The question itself—the fact that it has been asked—

lends credence to Ortega's idea of perception. The images of the four great storytellers' protagonists, from the hallucinating knight to the superannuated Patriarch and Big Mama's corpse bubbling over in tropical heat until the Pope arrives, belong to our confused age as well as to their own.

10
Martí, Vasconcelos, Mistral:
Commitment as Art

JOSÉ MARTÍ, JOSÉ VASCONCELOS, AND GABRIELA MISTRAL THOUGHT OF literature as a process naturally connected to social and political activity. They were aware that in one way or another all writers function politically. The writer's political participation, whether intentional or simply coincidental, is real and self-generating, because all writers seek the *privileges of power* inherent to seeing and hearing things in perspectives favorable to their art. They also recognized (as Cervantes, Dostoevsky, Borges, and García Márquez consistently have done) the power of memory to function in creative ways.

When conscientiously exercised, the privileges of power illuminate important experiences and problems, and convey in particular rhythms and images one's hopes and compulsions. Writers and political leaders begin with a feeling of what—beyond publication or election—they want to achieve. Inevitably, they seek collaboration in the process. Just as political leaders depend on a constituency, writers need to involve their readers and hope to attract critical attention. And, like the best (i.e., ethically and socially responsible) political leaders, the best writers seek to educate.

José Martí ("el apóstol"), José Vasconcelos ("Ulises criollo"), and Gabriela Mistral ("la maestra rural") were educators in the broadest and deepest sense. They expressed themselves as reformers and father-and-mother figures in the culture of their respective nations and consistently called for a more spiritually united and historically enlightened Hispanic America. Like Rubén Darío, Martí and Mistral acquired fame principally for their verse; but all three of these poets were also creative journalists and published more articles and essays than poems. For his part Vasconcelos, the inherent polemicist, always opted for prose; but the Mexican "Creole Ulysses" (as he saw himself) was driven by a poetic temperament and in his *Etica* (1932) defines the philosopher as "a poet with a system."

Further, we should remember that Martí (Cuba, 1853), Vasconcelos (Mexico, 1883) and Mistral (Chile, 1889), wrote during Latin America's transition from its nineteenth-century colonialist hangover to twentieth-century political adventurism. The future was their growing obsession. They saw their respective countries as inseparable parts of a continent in the making, and eloquently expressed their concepts of what Hispanic-American culture and civilization in the modern world should be. Their convictions were their stimulation: the self-sufficient Hispanic-American spirit of Martí's "Our America," Vasconcelos's "The Cosmic Race," and Mistral's essays on "feminine patriotism" as the equivalent of "Perfect Maternity." The literary renovation that gave expression to these aspirations began, of course, with Martí.

MARTÍ, THE POET IN NEW YORK

At a symposium at the University of Miami in 1990, I heard the late novelist Reinaldo Arenas read an essay, "The Blessed 1960s" ("Los dichosos años sesenta"). It was a displaced person's lament directed at an audience of mostly fellow Cuban exiles. Arenas based his presentation on impressions of a recent train ride in the eastern United States. He referred to a previous lecture he'd been in the process of writing on that same trip, a paper in praise of the epoch-making Hispanic-American novels of the 1960s. His enthusiasm for the novels and, more generally, the more hopeful and vibrant spirit of the decade in which they appeared was in contrast to the "suffocating North American landscape" he had seen from the train window in 1989. In that spectacle he found little more than an uninspiring repetition of the same lines of utility poles, and a redundant architecture of service stations and fast-food places.

More than a literary landscape, of course, Arenas's piece was the echoing of a state of mind, a dark and very subjective reflection on the Cuban condition of exile, a shared—as he put it—"condemnation of memory and disillusionment." Hearing his strangely lyrical lament led me to wonder what José Martí would have said, had his life begun a century later, and had he witnessed the same scenario that Arenas was complaining about.

Anachronistic as the comparison appears, the question of what Martí, or another Martí, might have written in our time is a valid one. As well as illuminating similarities and differences between the rambunctious, enterprising North American Gilded Age of the 1880s and 1890s and a fuzzier, still more Avaricious Age of a century later, the comparison increases Martí's already high relevance to the contemporary world. His situation was similar to Arenas's in the broad historical sense that both wrought their writing from a labyrinth of social and cultural instabilities, and in the more specific biographical sense that both were exiles and victims of political oppression. But in those sacrificial roles they differed significantly. In almost all he wrote after *El mundo alucinante* (1969), his symbolic resurrection of the Mexican independence activist Friar Servando Teresa de Mier, Arenas implied that through fantasy, the subversion of conventions and an ironic combination of narrative voices, literature had become—for him—the only form possible of Cuban liberation. By contrast Martí was a dedicated revolutionary, political organizer, and poetic journalist and actively practiced his quest for Cuban liberation in the real world. It could be said in retrospect that Martí's literary power had three components: the generating forces of hope, cultural curiosity, and a sense of mission.

The United States, from the winter of 1880 to the winter of 1895, was his cultural proving ground, the turbulent environment centered mainly in New York that simultaneously attracted and estranged him. Everything around him awoke his curiosity. In a single open letter of the hundreds he published in *La Nación* of Buenos Aires—one dated in New York, April 23, 1885—he combines his view of the alienating atmosphere of North American life with a reference to a young man's suicide after murdering his mother and sister at the beach, a definition of heroism, recent innovations in university education, portrait painting in the United States compared to art in Mexico of the same period, and a collective characterization—on balance not very favorable—of American women.[1]

The bulk of his chronicles followed a similar pattern, the notes of a high-strung immediate witness. Geographically and politically the Cuban was an exile; personally he received the hospitality and notable affections of Carmen Miyares de Mantilla, who ran the boardinghouse in Brooklyn where he resided until his revolutionary sortie to

Cuba (via Florida and Haiti) on January 30, 1895. Simply put, Carmen became his real and ideal partner, literally replacing Carmen Zayas Bazán (the poet's offical and estranged wife who remained in Cuba and visited New York only once, in 1885). As José Miguel Oviedo demonstrates in *La niña de New York* (Mexico City: Fondo de Cultura Económica, 1989), Carmen Mantilla's daughter María Mantilla ("la niña" alluded to in the title) was also Martí's. María, in turn, would later marry and become the mother of movie actor César Romero. The impetus and unsettled nature of North American society energized the writer's democratic spirit. Martí's New York, especially, had an aura of magic reality, a Protean, kaleidoscopic manifestation of light, color, movement, sound, and gesture. As poet and essayist the Cuban was (in ways similar to Walt Whitman) the mirror and resonator of his surroundings. Ivan Schulman sees that kinetic quality as a fundamental attribute of Spanish American Modernism, the literary movement in full flower during Martí's productive years, that is, Hispanic *modernismo* as "the literary mode of a world in transformation, a universal metamorphosis that Martí perceived clearly."[2]

In an essay written during his first year in New York—one of three under the title "Impresiones de América" and waggishly subtitled in English for publication in *The Hour* "By a Very Fresh Spaniard"—he sets forth his view of North American life as a contradiction between the spirit of free initiative and a strange lack of feeling. On July 10, 1880 he wrote:

> At last I've found a country where everybody seems to be his own master. One can breathe freely, since here freedom is the foundation, shield and essence of life. Here one can be proud of his species. Everyone works, everyone reads. But does everyone feel with same intensity that he reads and works? . . . This feverish life; this astonishing movement; this splendid yet ailing nation, on the one hand marvelously extended, on the other—that of intellectual pleasure—puerile and poor; this colossal and candid giant; these women too richly dressed to be happy; these men, too obsessed with filling their pockets to concern themselves with spiritual matters—it all comes to my lips simultaneously and begins to take shape in this brief account of my impressions. (*Obras completas,* 19:106 and 109).

Martí, who by 1880 had spent time in Spain, Guatemala, and Mexico, added in the "Impressions of America" just quoted: "Never had

I experienced surprise in any country I visited before. Here I was surprised." The stimulus of surprise would not fade with his first impressions. Later a Sunday visit to Coney Island and its colorful distractions, the demeanor and diet of John L. Sullivan, who in 1889 was to win the last bare-knuckled boxing championship in seventy-five rounds, and the commencement ceremony at Harvard in 1886 were equally vivid revelations. On Harvard's graduating class he wrote:

> Ah! How one envies the scope of instruction at Harvard, where no subject worthy of the mind lacks a good teacher. . . . And yet, what flower can live without air? All those professorial qualities, all that luxury of courses and professors, all the educators' glorious determination to apply what they teach to the times in which those who have grown up will now have to live—all that seems to evaporate in an atmosphere too heavy for souls that seem to perish for lack of stimulation in this crazy struggle for simple pecuniary gain, that are immobilized by their disdain for hard earned careers, clean careers of modest production. They're the preformed sons of these steely-eyed and insecure men whose only true ideal—the ability to rake in a huge fortune quickly—surpasses any concern for humanity or for their country.[3]

Literary historians have written mostly on Martí's poetry and the modernistic luxury of his language, undeniably one of the richest in Spanish since Luis de Góngora's in the seventeenth century. For the same reason and recently maybe more so because of late-twentieth-century academic readers' fashionable emphasis on self-reflecting texts, his main function as a journalist—admittedly one with several muses whispering in his ear—has been slighted. As serious readers of Hispanic-American literature we might recognize that newspaper writing, particularly in the nineteenth century when it tended to be more subjective, is quite compatible with "creative" writing. Had Tolstoy, Dickens, and Pérez Galdós not also had the investigative compulsions of good reporting, they probably would have been literary failures. Their great aesthetic talent as fundamental Hispanic *modernistas* notwithstanding, the Nicaraguan Darío, the Uruguayan José Enrique Rodó, and Martí also stood out as witnesses of their era; and of the three Martí was the most responsive to life as a multiple and changeable phenomenon.

Over a half-century ago Pedro Henríquez Ureña classified Martí's prose as mainly journalism and observed that his most frequent form was the *crónica* which, it can be added, has a had a vital function in Hispanic America in every century since the Conquest, within works as varied as Bernal Díaz del Castillo's *Historia de la conquista de México,* Domingo F. Sarmiento's *Facundo,* Martí's *Escenas norteamericanas,* Elena Poniatowska's *La noche de Tlatelolco* and Eduardo Galeano's *Memoria del Fuego.* Henríquez Ureña's definition of the *crónica* as Martí practiced it was "a commentary on some event of the present; when sent from a foreign country it had to include all kinds of occurrences: a railroad catastrophe or an art exposition, a financial crisis, a recently opened play or new book, the killing of Jesse James and the construction of the Brooklyn Bridge: a form of literary journalism unknown before 1870 and no longer fashionable. It tended to be superficial if the author also was."[4] Of course, Martí was often carried away by his descriptive enthusiasm, but his prose was always luminous and lyrical and his vision was never superficial.

The Gilded Age in the United States was the period between the Civil War and the late nineteenth century noted for its industrial growth, social opulence, and a fondness for things superficially attractive—an era in which inventions, artificial substances like Coca-Cola and commercial innovations abounded and the Standard Oil Company, founded in 1879, the Vanderbilt and Morgan families, Boss Tweed, and Jay Gould got away with what in a later time the Enron, World Com, and Halliburton Corporations would like to have gotten away with unnoticed. In a more positive vein, Samuel Eliot Morrison writes, "for all the corruption and pitiful politics of the Gilded Age, it was a robust, fearless, generous era, full of gusto and the joy of living, affording wide scope to individual energy and material creation."[5] The era included Mark Twain—coauthor with Charles Dudley Warner of a political *roman a clef* titled *The Gilded Age* (1873) as well as creator of the great *Huckleberry Finn*—Walt Whitman and Ralph Waldo Emerson (the principal believers in the high potentials of the individual). Significantly, Martí wrote two of his finest essays, both perceptive literary portraits, on Emerson (1882) and Whitman (1887).

Immersed in the light, shadows and turmoil of his exile in the United States, José Martí never lost focus on the political and cultural situations of his native land as an integral part of Hispanic America. When he declared in his best-known essay "Nuestra América" (1891), that *"pensar es servir"* he wasn't implying submission or blind obedience. Rather, he was affirming, with prophetic intuition, the teacher's sense of ethical and social responsibility as it applied to Hispanic America's future. He noticed that, nearly a century after the wars for their political independence, Hispanic nations were still in the awkward process of securing cultural independence and each of them had to assert its function "of the republic that fights against colonial thinking." In "Nuestra América" Martí rejected "the excessive importation of foreign ideas and formulas." In his prescription for Hispanic America's collective self-reliance he accepted no dictator or caudillo, no form of oppression or censorship, no threat to one's individual freedom or welfare. For him, writing was always an act in behalf of the collective good.

José Vasconcelos: Politician and Writer

As Secretary of Public Education Vasconcelos invited Gabriela Mistral to participate in Mexico's new public school and library program, a function she fulfilled from 1922 to 1924. In testimony included in her notebooks, Gabriela remarks that she had little in common with most Mexican writers of the period. Two important exceptions were Alfonso Reyes, whom she had admired since the publication of *Visión de Anahuac* (1917) and with whom she was to form a lifetime friendship, and José Vasconcelos. Of the latter she wrote: "Vasconcelos has sufficed for me; he's the purest and most dignified representative of Mexican thought, the organizing and creative mind, and active leadership. A man of cultural spirit, religious sentiment and social ideals."[6]

Like Martí, José Vasconcelos was an activist with a hero's as well as a lover's intuitions. His restless image returns intermittently to Mexican political life, and invites comparison with Martí, and Latin America's other most memorable practicing idealist of the nineteenth century, Domingo Faustino Sarmiento. All three were militants in eras stimulated more by initiatives for the future than by past heritage. All three were educators in action as well as in spirit. As leaders and writers Sarmiento, Martí, and Vasconcelos were obsessed—respectively—with Argentina's, Cuba's, and Mexico's potential as nations and cultures. Vasconcelos could be defined as a temperament with a cause, quick to advocate and quick to condemn.

But the circumstances and outcomes of their lives were very different. Sarmiento died with the glow of a civic patriarch still around him. Martí died, an easy target in a poorly planned battle in eastern Cuba (shortly after disobeying General Máximo Gómez's order to retreat) on May 19,1895, hero and martyr of a not very well organized liberation. The political process then set in motion was only partly fulfilled later—successively scarred as it was by the Platt Amendment imposed by the United States in 1902, the authoritarian corruption under the regimes of Gerardo Machado and Fulgencio Batista, and Fidel Castro's unrelenting grip on power since 1959. For his part, Vasconcelos would experience—following his presidential campaign in 1929—a progressive loss of political prestige and would die of natural causes in 1959. It would be an understatement to call his election-day defeat (November 17, 1929) suspicious. For the officially declared victor (Pasucal Ortiz Rubio), and his supporters aided by the preceding president Plutarco Elías Calles, the outcome was legitimate. For virtually everyone else it was fraudulent. "I've been cheated, not defeated," he would tell an American reporter.[7] Years later, in the summer of 1958, Vasconcelos appeared on a weekly series of television programs in Mexico with the conservative Catholic poet Alfonso Junco and the leftist sociologist Jorge Carrión, and I recall how openly he expressed his political bitterness, only partly softened by his melancholy for the lost aspirations of his youth.

Fortunately for Mexican literature, the distractions and obstacles he began experiencing in 1925 (the year after he resigned as Secretary of Public Education), his political exile during the 1930s, and the resentments he felt from the early 1940s until his death did not weaken his dedication to writing. Rather, those problems stimulated him and gave his essays and autobiography extra force and vitality. His creative energy is aimed mainly at self-justification in the four volumes of his memoirs published between 1935 and 1939 (*Ulises criollo, La tormenta, El desastre,* and *El proconsulado*), in which his psychological motivation is comparable to that of Hernán Cortés's justifications in his letters to the Emperor of the Holy Roman Empire, Charles V, or those of Sarmiento and Simón Bolívar in their testimonies.[8]

Vasconcelos's temperamental inclinations sometimes led him to over-simplify reality. In his commentaries on the complicated process of the Mexican Revolution and the civil conflicts continually erupting from 1910 to 1930, as well as on history in general, he made black-and-white judgments when he should have seen differences in more ambiguous tones of gray. For example, in his prologue to *La raza cósmica* (1925) he judged Hispanic America's historic struggle in the world to be a "clash of Latinity against Saxonism," and thought that the alleged cultural inferiority of England (which he dubbed "The Island of Pirates") and the United States (whose inhabitants he saw simply as materialistic "Anglo-Saxons") was the determining factor behind England's and the United States' economic and diplomatic support of Mexican dictators Porfirio Díaz and Victoriano Huerta and strongman Plutarco Elías Calles. That cultural inferiority was also evident, he claimed, in the Yankees' cuisine, insipid like their Protestant religion and unromantic social mores.

In a more positive vein, he believed that the Ideal was attainable only through good education, and that barbarism proceeded directly from ignorance. In his "Discurso del maestro" (1923) and in several passages of his memoirs he opposes the image of Quetzalcoatl, the mythical civilizing hero who disappeared several years before the Spanish conquest, to the specter of Huitzilopochtli, the violent god of war. "Today," he proclaimed, "the collective conscience will take inspiration from Quetzalcoatl, whose soul multiplies in each one of our teachers." José Vasconcelos "Discurso pronunciado el 'Día del Maestro,'" in *Discursos, 1920–1950* (Mexico City: Ediciones Botas, 1950), p. 113. Vasconcelos spoke on that occasion as Secretary of Public Education, a position he held from 1921 to 1924 and in which he organized the first nationwide public school system in Mexico, founded public libraries, and subsidized the mural art program and the publication of textbooks and classics of history and literature for free distribution. His tenure as Secretary of Education proved to be his greatest intellectual and cultural contribution to Mexico. He was repeating, in effect, the formula that Sarmiento expounded ("civilization versus barbarity.") in his biography of Juan Facundo Quiroga.

Vasconcelos viewed history through the initiatives and limitations of its individuals. He disdained the masses and most of their uncultured military leaders. Consequently, he underestimated the anonymous forces that motivated the impoverished and dispossessed, the same forces that Mariano Azuela, writing in the heat of the Revolution, fully recognized in his novel *Los de abajo* (1916). For the author of *Ulises Criollo*, observed his reader and critic José Joaquín Blanco in his book *Se llamaba Vasconcelos* (1980), "only individuals have meaning, the masses amount to something less than a geographical setting." (José Joaquín Blanco, *Se llamaba Vasconcelos. Una evocación crítica* [Mexico City: Fondo de Cultura Económica, 1980], 63).

Vasconcelos's multifaceted will power—political, amatory, philosophical, social, pedagogic, aesthetic—swept him toward curious extremes and prejudices. In an interview I had with him in July, 1958 in Mexico City he emphasized the motives for his bitterness: the National University of Mexico, which as its rector in 1920 he had given the motto "Por mi raza hablará el espíritu" ("Our spirit speaks in behalf of my race"), had fallen prey to materialists, "Jews," and communist sympathizers; Mexico had lost sight of Spain's sixteenth-century religious mission that was the guiding spirit of the Conquest; most North Americans had mistakenly rejected Senator Joseph McCarthy's anticommunist crusade; the Mexican Revolution, in which as a young idealist he had energetically participated, had ended as a useless mess, etc. He had become a reactionary in the fullest sense.

The resentments he expressed that day in 1958, less than a year before his death, had been simmering since 1940, when he founded in Mexico City *El Timón*, a short-lived ultraconservative journal whose editorials called for a new Christian crusade and expressed open admiration for Hitler, Mussolini, and Franco. Nevertheless, that same force of will in all its distortions had always reinforced his literary visions. As Sarmiento had previously done in Argentina, Vasconcelos reached his major cultural achievements (particularly as Secretary of Public Education) and wrote his best work before 1940. From the start, Apollo and Dionysus struggled within him. On one hand, he esteemed the principles of aesthetic proportion and symmetry, for example in his succinct, sometimes oversimplified *La raza cósmica* (1925) and his longer, sometimes rambling *Estética* (1935). On the other hand, he submitted to the impetuous spirit that dominated his political and civic activism of the 1920s.

Further, Vasconcelos simultaneously lived his amorous and political passions. His love for Elena Arizmendi Mejía ("Adriana" in *Ulises criollo*, "Eva gloriosa" in *La tormenta*), whom he met in 1911, coincided with his energetic support for the short-lived administration of Francisco I. Madero, assassinated in February 1913 by secret order of his successor, Victoriano Huerta. Adriana would then be with him during most of his exile over the next seven years. She had become, at the same time, a metaphor of infinite love and the guiding spirit

behind his patriotism. It could be said that both Vasconcelos's intimate relationship with Elena Arizmendi and his intense political activity were based on a kind of utopian ecstasy. Accordingly, the
image of "Adriana" revisited him as he wrote *Ulisis criollo* years later.
Writing that first volume of the memoirs was his way of reliving the
ecstasy.

The relationship with "Valeria"—in real life, Antonieta Rivas Mercado (1900–1931)—was less erotic, yet perhaps more intense for its
natural convergence of political and literary passions. Rightfully,
Vasconcelos dedicated the fourth volume of his memoirs, *El proconsulado* (1939) to "doña A.R.M., and all those who fell in the cause
of a regenerated Mexico."[9] José Vasconcelos, *El proconsulad.* (Mexico
City: Editorial Trillas, 1998), p. 27. Antonieta was heir to a family
fortune and the daughter of a prestigious architect, Antonio Rivas
Mercado. She was a principal adviser in Vasconcelos's presidential
campaign, and in Paris a few days before her death he told her, "You
are the homeland that accompanies me." As he would later recall,
"In Valeria I found an extension of my own conscience." But on
February 11, 1931 Antonieta walked to the front pew in the Cathe-
dral of Nôtre Dame and shot herself through the head. Her suicide
appears to have been motivated at least in part by her divorced status
since 1927 and the instability of her relationships with Vasconcelos
and the Mexican painter Manuel Rodríguez Lozano. Some irony is
to be found in her use of Vasconcelos's pistol—which she took se-
cretly from his dresser the same day she killed herself.[10] The suicide
ended a vibrant life; it was also an appropriate symbol for the end of
the *vasconcelista* movement in Mexico. Antonieta was a romantic
figure, personally and publicly, who in the 1920s had been passion-
ately devoted to her work as theatrical promoter, actress, and cam-
paigner. She was also a talented author, and had she lived beyond
her thirty years would have achieved literary fame. In *El proconsulado*
Vasconcelos includes several samples of her writing: "Mexico in
1928," "José de León Toral" (on Alvaro Obregón's assassin) and
"Germán del Campo." And a long letter that Antonieta wrote to Gabriela Mistral was reproduced, under the title "Vasconcelos frente
al imperialismo," in *Diario de Panamá* on March 6, 1930.[11]

In a vignette of Vasconcelos in his memoirs, *El río: Novelas de caballería* (1986) the Guatemalan poet and art critic Luis Cardoza y Aragón calls him "brilliant, imperious, resentful and unbearable." Luis
Cardoza y Aragón, *El río: Novelas de caballería* (Mexico City: Fondo de

Cultura Económica, 1986, 711). Cardoza clearly perceived the rest-lessness and contradictions of an activist writer given to thinking in absolute terms. Probably the restlessness and contradictions were the result of a vibrant inner energy that Vasconcelos himself called "spiritual," strongly suggesting that his ethics and aesthetics—based more on desire than on reality—were inseparable from his political action.

The chapter "En provincia" in *Ulises criollo* contains passages that underscore the absolutist nature of the author's thought. In "En provincia" he dances a virtual waltz with irrationality, rejecting the "empirical discipline" he attributes to "Anglo-Saxon minds" as dif-ferent as those of Herbert Spencer and John Dewey, and declares: "Let's deny all consummated actions and accede to potentiality swelled with surprise." José Vasconcelos, "En provincia," *Ulises crio-llo*" (Mexico City: Editorial Trillas, 1998, 257). In the section "La composición, último fin de la estética" of *Estética* he stresses the reli-gious nature of his concept of beauty: "Artistic composition strives to use universal elements as signs of a language that expresses quali-ties of the Absolute." That's what, he believes, liturgies were made for, and why liturgy is "the ultimate and highest form of the Fine Arts." José Vasconcelos, *Estética*, 3rd ed. (Mexico City: Ediciones Botas, 1945), 273. It was in that light—a liturgy that became a cru-sade—that he saw his presidential campaign of 1929.

Although he was no admirer of Unamuno (who he believed was a philosophical "dilettante" suffering from Kierkegaard's "mental poverty") he seems to share the Spaniard's intuitions expressed in *Del sentimiento trágico de la vida*. *El proconsulado*, like the other three volumes of his memoirs, exudes a tragic sentiment of its own.[12] The memoirs are, basically, his *missa solemnis* for the democratic process in Mexico, which during and following the 1929 campaign he be-lieves succumbed to corrupt interests.

Let the title and spirit of Schopenhauer's masterwork, *The World as Will and Idea*, serve as a prologue to Vasconcelos's life and writing. As it did for Martí, literary expression for Vasconcelos evolved as the articulation of an overriding purpose: the cultural regeneration of his country. But the unquiet Mexican proved to be a temperamental philosopher as well as a "poet with a system." Accordingly—and in the context of Schopenhauer's thought—his *will* manifested itself as both his strength and his weakness. In its intensity it affected every-thing—political, amatory, religious, cultural—that he was involved in, and sometimes exceeded rational limits. His *idea* was the "Spirit" that only he could have transformed into literary settings as varied as the utopian fantasies of *La raza cósmica*, the recollected nights of a perpetually displaced lover, and wide-ranging. His sustained exercise of that spirit was the direct cause of his political downfall and the ultimate victory of his written work.

GABRIELA MISTRAL: THE MATERNAL VOICE

In a 1945 essay written on the occasion of Gabriela Mistral's winning that year's Nobel Prize for Literature, the Argentine author and editor Victoria Ocampo wrote that her Chilean contemporary had "three great loves: poetry, children, and the American [i.e., Latin American] continent." Ocampo's essay is included in her *Testimonios*, (Victoria Ocampo "Grabriela Mistral y el premio Nobel," *Testimonios*, vol. 3 [Buenos Aires: Editorial Sudamericana, 1946], 3:171). Mistral's three loves are evident throughout her written work, especially that of children. "*Mis niños*" is an expression she applies generically to children everywhere, with special concern for those of her own country and Latin America. Further, the significance and sentiment she attributes to the word "children" extends to indigenous peoples, "*mestizos*," the impoverished, the unprotected and—wherever they are—the dispossessed.

She was never to marry or give birth, but from youth to her last days Gabriela Mistral expressed herself as a Mother. In her introduction to *Lecturas para mujeres* (1924) she categorically declares that in her view "feminine patriotism means perfect maternity" and "the most patriotic education given to women is, therefore, that which emphasizes the meaning of family." In the 1920s when it became a burning issue, she supported women's suffrage, specifying at the same time that a "parliament of women" would be no more acceptable than the traditionally established ones of men. In 1928 in Paris she heard and praised a proposal that congresses and parliaments be composed of "guild" representatives. "I would gladly listen to a delegate of seamstresses, of elementary school teachers, of all the workers in the shoe industry, describe their trades candidly and in person."[13] Years later, her concept of woman's role in modern life would displease many critics and readers of the feminist persuasion.

In the same introduction (1924) to *Lecturas para mujeres* she declared that woman's only reason for existing in the world was maternity, "material and spiritual, or just the latter for those of us who don't have children." One critic, Doris Meyer, considers this view of maternity a serious limitation and compares it to that of "the Fascist leaders [Mistral] so vehemently hated later on."[14]

By current guidelines Gabriela Mistral (born Lucila Godoy Alcayaga) was not a feminist, yet she shared the feminists' concerns over education, human rights, world peace, imperialism, and totalitarianism. She was also a fervent Pan-Americanist in the spirit of Bolívar, Martí, and Augusto César Sandino (each of whom she praised in essays). It could be recognized, particularly in her case, that in the continuous debate over the status of the sexes, maternity is not in all cases a concept to be rejected. Maternal nature is—as the poet and editor Donald Hall reminds us—"*another survival of infancy* [my emphasis], like most of the things that make a poem."[15]

In his introduction to a chapter on Chilean poetry (originally published in 1893) Marcelino Menéndez y Pelayo writes that in Chile "a tribe of heroic barbarians wore out the swords and patience of their conquerors and determined the austere and virile physiognomy of that colony." He continues: "The character of the Chilean people, like that of their partly Basque progenitors, is positive, practical, prudent, not inclined to idealities." As if that weren't enough, he concludes that the dogmatic positivism then dominant in Chilean schools had contributed to "the habitual aridity of Chilean literature, generally solid, but seldom appealing." Marcelino Menéndez y Pelayo, *Historia de la poesía hispano-americana*, Enrique Sánchez Reyes, ed. (Santander: Consejo Superior de Investigaciones Científicas, 1948, 2:219, 298).

Unperceptive amidst his grandiloquence, Don Marcelino was a poor prophet for Chile's future culture and literature. The imminent "Republic of Poets" would be born precisely with the early verses of Gabriela Mistral (herself a direct descendant of the heroic barbarians and practical Basques that Menéndez Pelayo had commented on) and would thrive in the works of Neruda, Vicente Huidobro, Humberto Díaz-Casanueva, Gonzalo Rojas, Jorge Tellier, and beyond. On receiving the Nobel prize in November, 1945 Gabriela gave full recognition to her origins and identity: "I come from peasants and am one myself" and "I'm the direct voice of the poets of my race and the indirect voice of two noble languages: Spanish and Portuguese."

Gabriela was born the same year (1889) as Charlie Chaplin and the authors, respectively, of *Zein und Zeit, Ultima Tule, Les Enfants terribles*, and *Mein Kampf.* The biographical coincidence is significant. One can understand Mistral's life and work better in the light (and shadows) of Chaplin's compassionate and socially sensitive shenanigans, the existential anguish commented on in Martin Heidegger's philosophy, the lucid historical and cultural intuitions of Alfonso Reyes relating to "la inteligencia americana," the poet-angel's vision of world chaos in Jean Cocteau's novel, and the bizarre concepts of human nature in Hitler's "essay." Gabriela alternated her awareness of the forces underlying these conflicting twentieth-century attitudes with her most intimate lyrical adventures.

She was a poet of deep affinities (with Dante, the Spanish mystics, Sor Juana Inés de la Cruz, children, José Martí, trees, mountains, the summer air) and, despite numerous contacts with friends, officials, and other writers, an exhaustive solitude. Her personal life was an accumulation of sorrows. It included an errant father, harsh deceptions in school, an early unrequited love that ended in suicide and was the main stimulus for her first book of poetry, *Desolación* (1922), and (in 1943) the death—probably also by suicide—of a nephew. The result of all this was her permanently tragic view of life. The misfortunes of the person, Lucila Godoy Alcayaga, invaded the spirit of the poet, Gabriela Mistral.

Lucila was scarcely three when her father abandoned home. He was a teacher, part-time poet, and a spiritual brother of Laura's father in Tennessee Williams's *The Glass Menagerie*, the obscure telephone company employee who "fell in love with long distance" and left home for good. At the age of eight she was falsely accused of robbing paper from the storeroom in her school, and stoned by her classmates on her way home the same afternoon. Years later she was dismissed from the Escuela Normal de Serena for having written (under the probable influence of Camille Flammarion) that "nature is God."

After her close collaboration with Vasconcelos on the educational projects in Mexico, the poet traveled to Europe in 1924, and to Central America and the United States in 1930 and 1931. For the indiscretion of declaring herself an antifascist in Mussolini's Italy in 1932, she was dismissed from her position as Chilean consul in Genoa.

Nevertheless, she continued serving in consular posts in Spain, Portugal, Guatemala, the United States, Mexico, and Brazil. It was in Rio de Janeiro that her fifteen-year-old nephew, (whom she had cared for and educated from his infancy) died. Thus, the Nobel Prize, two years later, came as a limited joy. She died, after a prolonged and painful illness, in Hempstead, Long island, on January 10, 1957.

It seems strange and unjust that this dynamic writer, whose poetry is given to us in verse and also in the prose she called "Messages" (*Recados*), "Celebrations" (*Elogios*), and "Topics" (*Materias*), has been largely ignored by academic critics in recent decades. Or perhaps it's a blessing in disguise that her fate rests in the memory of miscellaneous and anonymous readers, and not in the manipulations of scholars attracted by models more amenable to scholarly discussion. The current academic tendency to bypass or ignore Gabriela Mistral coincides with many theorists' tendency to concentrate on *each other's discourses* more than on the poems, novels, stories, plays and essays that are supposed to be the primary objects of their attention. Independent as she was of twentieth-century movements and trends (postmodernism, the vanguards, surrealism, antipoesía, etc.), she didn't qualify—like Vallejo, Huidobro, Borges, Girondo, Neruda, and Paz—as one of Saúl Yurkievich's *fundadores*.[16] In his posthumous memoirs *Confieso que he vivido* (1974), Pablo Neruda recalls that as his secondary-school teacher in Temuco, southern Chile, Gabriela gave him Russian novels whose turbulent visions remained with him the rest of his life, and that for him "she always had a good companion's open smile, a white-flour smile on a dark-bread face." Pablo Neruda, *Confieso que he vivido* (Caracas: Seix Barral, 1974, 393).

Possibly her most suggestive portrait is that of her long-time Mexican friend, Palma Guillén. It appears in the brief preface that Guillén wrote for the 1967 edition of Mistral's *Lecturas para mujeres* (1922–24): "For me, then a conceited young woman, she seemed unattractively dressed, poorly girdled; with skirts that were too long, flat-soled shoes, and her hair in a low bun. I still see Gabriela's timorous eyes. Those eyes—almost always half-closed—had two ways of looking. One was quick and lightening-like, whether due to fascination, surprise, anger or fear; the other was serene, sustained, like still water—green water with a lot of light in it, the look of confidence, understanding and repose. But, most of the time, her eyes were like frightened birds" (in Gabriela Mistral, *Lecturas para mujeres*, 6th ed. [Mexico City: Editorial Porrúa, 1980], v–vi).

The "two ways of looking" (apprehensive and confident) applied to what she wrote. Her world was inhabited by magical as well as real beings. One of her most inspired poems—"La flor del aire" (included in *Tala*, 1938)—is a dream in which she encounters a mysterious "governess" or spirit on a meadow who orders her to carry out a series of searches for flowers.

"La flor del aire" is a metaphor for life as an endless quest for beauty; it is also the author's affirmation that poetry is spiritual dedication, something rooted in one's sense of mission. The phantasmal figure on the meadow has commanded her to gather and carry *all* the flowers she finds, and to follow her (her muse, guide, and goddess) in fulfillment of her designated mission as long as she lives. Poetry, from her earliest compositions to the last, was Gabriela's natural instrument for expressing maternal love, the nostalgias of her homeland, and her educational and ideological commitments.

Like Martí and Vasconcelos, Gabriela did not hesitate to criticize the United States' Latin American policy when she thought it was mistaken or unjust. Three of her "Recados" (first published between March 1928, and June 1931) are a vigorous defense of Augusto César Sandino, the Nicaraguan revolutionary leader eventually to be murdered by order of Anastasio Somoza, against the imperialist policies of Calvin Coolidge and Herbert Hoover. In her insightful "La lengua de Martí" she reminds us that one of the Cuban poet's primary powers was his "tropicalism" (i.e., his expressive abundance, his warmth of spirit), a term which North Americans have traditionally interpreted as a motivation for political suspicion or an indication of cultural inferiority.

In personal encounters, as well as in her letters and published writing, Gabriela Mistral consistently said what she thought. Soon after receiving the Nobel Prize for literature in 1945 she traveled to Washington; and the poet Humberto Díaz-Casanueva, then Chile's ambassador to the United States, escorted her to a brief meeting with President Truman at the White House. During the polite exchanges called for on such occasions, the ambassador noticed his compatriot's growing impatience, and before long she blurted out, "Mr. President, don't you think it's terrible that such a cruel and bloody dictator as Trujillo remains in power in the Dominican Republic?"

As might be expected, Truman remained silent, limiting himself to a smile. But the poet-laureate hadn't finished, and added: "I'd like to ask you a favor, Mr. President; a country as prosperous as the one you lead should help my little Latin American Indians, who are so poor that they're hungry and can't go to school." Díaz-Casanueva concluded as follows, "Truman smiled again without saying anything; the Ambassador was nervous and so was the Chief of Protocol. There had to be an escape. . . . So they called in a photographer, who said, 'You all should be looking at the President with a smile.' And that's how we appeared for posterity."[17]

That nervous encounter dressed in forced smiles reflects, one could say, the basic lack of cultural and political communication that has spoiled North and Hispanic-American relations for nearly two centuries. Few have been as keenly aware of that problem as José Martí, José Vasconcelos, and Gabriela Mistral.

Notes

FOREWORD

1. Ortega y Gasset, *La dehumanización del arte y otros ensayos etéticos*, 5th edition (Madrid: Revista de Occidente, 1925).

2. See Patricia Rosas Lopátegui, *Testimonios sobre Elena Garro* (Monterrey: Ediciones Castillo, 2002), and the work of Elena Garro's and Octavio Paz's daughter, Helena Paz Garro, *Memorias* (Mexico City: Oceano, 2003).

CHAPTER 1. FIGURE AND FUNCTION

1. My translation, from José Martí, *Martí por Martí*, ed. Salvador Bueno (Mexico: Prensa Latinoamericana, 1982), 319.

2. Do ambiguities culminate as paradoxes in modern times? In an illustrated "annotation" ("American Lucifer: The Tormented Face of Osama bin Laden") in the December 2001 issue of *Harper's Magazine*, Bill Wasik comments, "Where our news media would have us see a devil from the East, a sneering emissary of Islamic fanaticism, we instead meet a gaze both familiar and empathetic. His demeanor is cordial—never grim, never fierce—even as he makes threats on our lives." (52)

3. Earlier in the same paragraph in which Cervantes asserts his step-fatherhood, he characterizes his Quijano/Quijote as "a dried offspring, wizened, fanciful and full of diverse thoughts . . . like someone who has grown up in a prison." A vibrant refutation *a priori* of Foucault's shortsighted definition. No one could have said it better than the gifted Stepfather.

CHAPTER 2. PÉREZ GALDÓS

1. Jacques Barzun, *Classic, Romantic and Modern*, 2nd ed. (University of Chicago Press, 1975), 56.

2. Carlos Ollero, "Galdós y Balzac," in *Benito Pérez Galdós*, ed. Douglass M. Rogers, (Madrid: Taurus, 1973), 190.

3. Victor Brombert, introduction to Honoré de Balzac, *La Peau de chagrin* (New York: Dell Publishing Co., 1962), 19.

4. Ricardo Gullón, "La historia como material novelable," in *Benito Pérez Galdós*, 409, 414.

5. On the occasion of Queen Mercedes' death in 1878, Federico Bravo Morata refers to the intensive efforts to find a new wife and "adequate royal choice" for

Alfonso XII and Spain: "El hombre moderno no puede menos que sonreír, siquiera íntimamente, cuando conoce estas andanzas de ministros y diplomáticos buscando una princesa para un monarca, repartiendo sus actividades convencionales con estas otras más próximas al celestineo que a la política." *Fin del siglo y de las colonias* (Madrid: Fenicia, 1972), 42.

6. Benito Pérez Galdós, *Obras completas*, vol. 3 (Madrid: Aguilar, 1961), 1361. Cited in text hereafter as *OC*.

7. Robert Ricard, "Mito, sueño y realidad en *Prim*," *Cuadernos Hispanoamericanos*, no. 250–52 (Oct. 1970–Jan. 1971), 340–55.

8. Walter T. Pattison, *Benito Pérez Galdós* (Boston: Twayne Publishers, 1975), 86.

9. Emile Zola, *Le Roman experimental* (Paris: Garnier-Flammarion, 1971), 64.

10. Ibid., 61.

11. José Schraibman, "Los sueños en *Fortunata y Jacinta*," in *Benito Pérez Galdós*, 163.

12. Antonio Sánchez Barbudo, "Torquemada y la muerte," in *Benito Pérez Galdós*, 351–63.

13. Pattison, *Benito Pérez Galdós*, 102.

CHAPTER 3. OCTAVIO PAZ

1. *El mono gramático* first appeared in Paris, in French, in 1972, but the original version, in Spanish, was not published until 1974.

2. Octavio Paz, "El mono gramático," in *Poemas, 1935–1975* (Barcelona: Seix Barral, 1979), 580–81.

3. Octavio Paz, "Nota," in *Puertas al campo*, 2nd ed. (México: Universidad Nacional Autónoma de México, 1967), 6–7

4. Octavio Paz, "Aniversario español," July 19, 1951, in *El ogro filantrópico* (Barcelona: Seix-Barral, 1979), 203.

5. According to Alfredo Roggiano ("Persona y ámbito de Octavio Paz" in *Octavio Paz* [Madrid: Editorial Fundamentos, 1979], 10–11) and Pablo Neruda (*Confieso que he vivido: Memorias* [Caracas: Seix-Barral, 1974], 182), Paz was in Spain, and also France, in 1937. Paz himself states, in a long footnote to his "Elegía a un compañero muerto en el frente de Aragón" in (*Poemas 1935–75*, 666–73), that he wrote the elegy in 1937, but also: "in 1938 I was in Spain—Barcelona, Valencia, the southern front—where a charismatic Mexican, Juan B. Gómez, commanded a brigade" (671).

6. Paz believes that in his foreign travels Ortega "was not a colonizer but a discoverer." ("José Ortega y Gasset: el cómo y el para qué," in *Hombres en su siglo y otros ensayos* [Barcelona: Seix-Barral, 1984] 98). If Paz means this in a figurative sense, with reference to the Spaniard's readings, he's right. But if Ortega's three sojourns in Argentina (in 1916, 1928, and 1939–42) are taken into account one has to disagree. In that country Ortega discovered virtually nothing of cultural significance and expressed or insinuated in several ways his desire to *colonize* immature intellectuals. On this relationship see chapter 5 of this book, "Ortega y Gasset in Argentina: The Exasperating Colony."

7. Octavio Paz, *El arco y la lira*, 2nd ed. (Mexico: Fondo de Cultura Económica, 1967), 264–65.

8. Pere Gimferrer, *Lecturas de Octavio Paz* (Barcelona: Editorial Anagrama, 1980), 61–62.

9. Published in Paz's *In/mediaciones* (Barcelona: Seix-Barral, 1979), 25–37. The passage quoted is from page 33.

10. See Octavio Paz, "México y los poetas del exilio español," in *Hombres en su siglo y otros ensayos* (Mexico City: Seix-Barral, 1984), 51.

11. Juan Gil Albert, *Los días están contados* (1974), quoted by Octavio Paz in *Hombres en su siglo, y otros ensayos* (Mexico City: Seix-Barral, 53–54). 53–54 (my translation).

12. See Rita Guibert, "Paz on Himself and His Writing: Selections from an Interview," in *The Perpetual Present: The Poetry and Prose of Octavio Paz*, Ivar Ivask, ed. (Norman: University of Oklahoma Press, 1974), 26.

13. The quotation from Machado appears as an epigraph for Chapter 1 (*"El pachuco y otros extremos"*) of Octavio Paz, *El laberinto de la soledad*, 2d ed. (Mexico City: Fondo de Cultura Económico, 1959), 7.

14. See note 6 above.

15. See Francisco Garfías, "Desvalorización de ideologies," *Excelsior* (July 7, 1991).

16. Jeremy Campbell, *Grammatical Man: Information, Entropy, Language and Life* (New York: Simon and Schuster, 1982), 84.

17. Octavio Paz, "La búsqueda del presente," in *Vuelta*, no. 170 (1990): 12.

18. Octavio Paz, *Los hijos del limo* (Barcelona: Seix Barral, 1974), 191.

19. Octavio Paz, *Vuelta* (Barcelona: Seix Barral, 1976), 79. Compare the first two lines (*La poesía no es la verdad:/ es la resurrección de presencias*) with the first two lines of Archibald MacLeish's poem quoted in the epigraph for this chapter (*A poem should be equal to:/ Not true*).

20. Abel Posse, *Daimón* (Barcelona: Plaza y Janés, 1989), 26.

21. Carlos Fuentes, *Casa con dos puertas* (México: Joaquín Mortiz, 1970), 156.

22. Quoted by Enrico Mario Santí in his introduction to *Primeras letras, (1931–43)*, Octavio Paz (México: Vuelta, 1988), 26.

23. "Introito a guisa de carpocapsa saltitans" [The allusion is to the discontinuous distribution (with "jumping paws") of Paz's introduction. That is, it leaps from pages 9–11 to157–59, back to 39–40, then forward to 260–65.] in A. Jiménez, *Nueva picardía mexicana*, 14th ed. (Mexico: Editores Mexicanos Unidos, 1979).

24. Octavio Paz, "Alrededores de la literature hispanoamericana," *In/mediaciones* (1976; Barcelona: Seix Barral, 1979), 28.

25. Octavio Paz, "Epistolario entre Ortega y Curtius," *Revista de Occidente*, no. 6 (1963): 341.

26. Octavio Paz, "Es moderna nuestra literatura?" in *In/mediaciones* (1975; Barcelona: Seix Barral, 1979), 43.

27. Octavio Paz, *El arco y la lira*, 2nd ed., (Mexico: Fondo de Cultura Económica, 1967), 265.

28. Some literary consequences of this phenomenon are discussed in chapter 9, "In and Out of Time."

29. Sexuality is the context in which this fusion is clearly evident. See Peter Earle, "Contextos y sextextos en Octavio Paz," in *Carnal Knowledge*, Pamela Bacarisse (Pittsburgh: Ediciones Tres Ríos, 1992), 83–89.

30. Octavio Paz, "Poesía e historia," in *Sombras de obras* (Barcelona: Seix Barral, 1983), 48. My translation.

CHAPTER 4. ON PICARESQUE PROGRESS

1. David Bosworth, "Echo and Narcissus: The Fearful Logic of Postmodern Thought," *Georgia Review* (Fall 1997: 414–15)

2. Claudio Guillén, "Toward a Definition of the Picaresque," in *Literature as System, Essays toward the Theory of Literary History* (Princeton: Princeton University Press, 1971), 71–106; reprinted in Gustavo Pellón and Julio Rodríguez-Luis (eds.), *Upstarts, Wanderers or Swindlers* (Amsterdam: Editions Rodopi B.V., 1986), 81–102.

3. Ulrich Wicks, "The Nature of Picaresque Narrative: A Modal Approach," *PMLA*, 84, no. 2 (1974): 249; reprinted in Pellón and Rodríguez Luis, 103–11.

Robert Alter, *Rogue's Progress: Studies in the Picaresque Novel* (Cambridge: Harvard University Press, 1964), and Alexander Blackburn, *The Myth of the Pícaro* (?).

4. Harry Sieber, *The Picaresque* (London: Methuen & Co., 1977), 57.

5. Pellón and Rodríguez-Luis, *Upstarts, Wanderers*, 100.

6. Harriet S. Turner, *Benito Pérez Galdós: Fortunata y Jacinta* (Cambridge University Press, 1992), 87.

7. See Nicholas Fraser and Marysa Navarro, *Eva Perón* (New York: W.W. Norton, 1980), 98.

8. Gabriel García Márquez, *Cien años de soledad* (Buenos Aires: Editorial Sudamericana, 1967), 204–5.

9. Carlos Fuentes, *La muerte de Artemio Cruz* (Caracas: Biblioteca Ayacucho, 1990), 72.

10. Ruben Dano, *Autobiografía* and *Oro de Mallorca* (Madrid: Mondadori, 1990), 41.

11. Charles D. Watland, *Poet Errant: A Biography of Rubén Darío* (New York: Philosophical Library, 1965), p. 57. Watland adds in a footnote that this incident did not occur—as Darío implied in his memoir—in 1889, but several years before.

12. José Rubén Romero, *La vida inútil de Pito Pérez*, in *Obras completas* (Mexico City: Editorial Porrua, 1979), 386.

13. Ibid., 14.

14. Quoted by Peter G. Earle, in "El arte de *El recurso del método*," *Academia Puertorriqueña de la Lengua Española*, 2, no. 7 (1975): 41.

15. Alejo Carpentier, *El recurso del método* (Mexico City: Siglo XXI, 1974), 91.

16. *El otoño del Patriarca* (Barcelona: Plaza & y Janés, 1975), 51.

17. Quoted by Ulrich Wicks, in Pellón and Rodríguez Luis, *Upstarts, Wanderers*, 110.

CHAPTER 5. ORTEGA Y GASSET

1. Francisco Romero, *Ortega y Gasset y el problema de la jefatura espiritual y otros ensayos* (Buenos Aires: Editorial Losada, 1960), 41–42.

2. Eduardo Mallea, *Historia de una pasión argentina*, 6th ed. (Madrid: Austral, 1969), 88.

3. Quoted by Antonello Gerbi in his illuminating book on European images of the New Word, *La disputa del Nuevo Mundo*, (Antonio Alatorre, trans.) (Mexico City: Fondo de Cultura Económica, 1960), 393.

4. Ortega y Gasset, "Hegel y América," in *Obras completas* (Madrid: Revista de Occidente, 1946), 569. Subsequent references to this edition are identified as *OC*.

5. They all appear (including "Hegel y América") in *Martinez Estrada, Meditación del pueblo joven y otros ensayos sobre América*, Paulino Garragori, ed. (Madrid: Alianza Editorial, 1981). Subsequent references to this edition are identified as *MPJ*.

6. Martínez Estrada's complete sentence from "Los valores" reads: "Our way of being is perhaps a spiritual form in a new world, where everything is yet to be accomplished, where much has been built to fill vacant properties, where buildings are occupied provisionally—in anticipation of their true owners' arrival." *Radiografía de la pampa*, ed. crítica, Leo Pollmann, Colección Archivos, no. 19, ALLCA 20 / Fondo de Cultura Económica, 1996, 249.

7. For Martínez Estrada's first commentary on Ortega see "El guaranguismo de Ortega y Gasset," in *Leer y escribir*, Enrique Espinoza, ed. (Mexico City: Joaquín Mortiz, 1969), 92–96.

8. Doris Meyer, *Victoria Ocampo: Against the Wind and the Tide* (New York: George Braziller, 1979), 60.

9. Alfonso Reyes, *Diario, 1911–1930*, Alicia Reyes, ed. (Guanajuato [Mexico]: Universidad de Guanajuato), 1969, 234.

10. Victoria Ocampo, "Quiromancia de la pampa," in *Testiomonios*, first series, 1920–1934 (Buenos Aires: Ediciones Fundacion Sur, 1981), 113.

11. Peter G. Earle, "Autobiography in the Latin American Essay," in *El ensayo hispánico*, Isaac J. Lévy and Juan Loveluck, eds., Hispanic Studies, no. 3 (Columbia: University of South Carolina Press, 1984), 139.

12. Barbara Bockus Aponte, *Alfonso Reyes and Spain* (Austin: University of Texas Press, 1972), 107.

13. Reproduced in Martínez Estrada's *Leer y escribir*, Enrique Espinoza, ed. (Mexico City: Joaquín Mortiz, 1969), 91–96.

14. "Problemas culturales," in *La Prensa*, August 15, 1911; reproduced in Ortega y Gasset, *Mocedades*, 2nd ed. (Buenos Aires: Colección Austral, 1943), 159–69.

15. In March, 1914, Ortega organized "La Liga de Educación Política Española." Its ninety-nine founding members included some big names: Manuel Azaña, Ricardo Baeza, Américo Castro, Enrique Díez Canedo, Antonio Machado, Ramiro de Maeztu, Salvador de Madariaga, Federico de Onís, Ramón Pérez de Ayala, Pedro Salinas. Ortega concludes the league's Manifesto (reproduced in *OC*, 270–71) as follows: "It's now time, then, to make an urgent call to our generation, and if no one positively qualified takes on the responsibility, then it's up to some lesser figure (like me) to do it."

16. See Alfonso Reyes's comment (previously referred to in this essay) in his diary entry for December 4, 1928. Ocampo, Reyes adds, was equally displeased with Ortega's philosophical disdain of music, "even though he goes to all the concerts; because he says what can't be *defined* has no *value*." (ibid.) Reyes, *Dario*, 234.

17. Martin S. Stabb, *In Quest of Identity* (Chapel Hill: University of North Carolina Press, 1967), 170–71.

18. Máximo Etchecopar, "Ortega, nuestro amigo," in *Historia de una afición a leer* (Buenos Aires: Editorial Universitaria de Buenos Aires, 1969), 78. Etchecopar mentions another testimony of this period that I haven't seen: Jaime Perriaux, *Algunas notas de conversaciones con Ortega* (La Plata: 1966).

19. Gregorio Marañon and Ramón Pérez de Ayala, "Manifiesto disolviendo la Agrupación al Servicio de la República," in *Luz* (October 29, 1932). Reproduced in Ortega, *OC*, 11:516–18.

20. Ortega y Gasset, "Epílogo para ingleses," in *La rebelión de las masas,* 36th ed. (Madrid: Revista de Occidente, 1962), 308 and 309.

21. See Patricio Canto, *El caso Ortega y Gasset* (Buenos Aires: Ediciones Leviatán, 1957), 108. Quoted by Carlos Rojas in his illuminating chapter on Ortega in *Diez figuras ante la Guerra Civil* (Barcelona: Ediciones Nauta, 1973), 343.

22. Ortega expressed his grievances and Ocampo seconded them in *Sur,* 7, no. 38 (Nov., 1937).

23. Neruda at the time was President of the Alianza. Ideologically and practically, of course, he was Ortega's opposite with regard to the political crises in Spain and Europe. See "Una declaración de la Alianza de Intelectuales de Chile para la Defensa de la Cultura," together with a reply from *Sur* with statements supporting *Sur*'s position from André Gide, André Malraux, André Maurois, Stefan Zweig, Aldous Huxley, and Hermann Keyserling in *Sur* 8, no. 41 (Feb., 1938): 79–85.

24. Pedro Henríquez Ureña, of the Dominican Republic, who emigrated to Argentina had begun teaching at the Colegio Nacional de la Universidad de La Plata in 1924, included in his "Caminos de nuestra historia literaria" (published in *Valoraciones* in the August and September issues of 1925) a section subtitled "América y la exuberancia," in which he rejected Ortega's thesis as stated in his letter to the young Argentine philosophy student. Henríquez Ureña writes: "I don't believe in the theory of our exhuberance. One could even go so far as to propose the opposite thesis; plenty of writers from the 16th century to the 20th could be named to prove it. My denial should not be taken as defensive. On the contrary, I ask: Are we considered and do we consider ourselves exuberant and emphatic, or ignorant and awkward? Ignorance, and all the ills stemming from it, are not characteristics; they're situations." The author then throws Ortega's emphasis theory, and Eugenio d'Ors's exuberance theory back at them. If by exuberance they meant fecundity, the prolific equivalents of Benito Perez Galdós or Emilia Pardo Bazán would be hard to find in Hispanic America. If they meant verbosity, no *criollo* could match Emilio Castelar or José Zorrilla or—for that matter—Victor Hugo, Byron, Espronceda, or Manuel José Quintana, none of whom came from the *petits pays chauds* of the New World.

25. Emilio A. Coni, "El hombre a la defensiva," *Nosotros,* 24, no. 251 (April, 1930), 46–56.

26. See Anderson Imbert, "Ortega y Gasset, politico, y la política," reproduced in *La flecha al aire* (Benoa Aires: Ediciones Gure, 1972), 65–68.

27. Ortega y Gasset, "El horizonte histórico," *OC,* 3:289–95. Of course, many others over the years have commented on Ortega's relationship with Argentina and Hispanic America. Consider, for example: José Luis Gómez Martínez distinguishes between "two" Ortegas: one facing the New World as he subjectively saw it; the other absorbed by abstract, philosophical issues. In general Gómez Martínez shares my view of Ortega's colonialist bias and aloofness from Argentine intellectuals. "Presencia de América en la obra de Ortega y Gasset," in *Quinto Centenario* (Madrid: Departamento de Historia, Universidad Complutense, June, 1983), 125–57.

German Gullón offers a good overview of the circumstances of Ortega's exile in "Desde el exilio: perspectiva intellectual de José Ortega y Gasset," *Los Ensayistas,* nos. 8–9 (University of Georgia, 1980), 23–35.

Elena Sansinena de Elizalde, an Argentine friend of Ortega's since 1916, quotes passages from his letters to her in 1936, 1937, and 1939 that poignantly reveal his depressed state as a displaced intellectual. See "Mi amistad con Ortega," *Sur,* no.

241 (July–August, 1956): 187–91. See also in this same "Homenaje a Ortega" issue of *Sur* twenty-nine other testimonies.

Victoria Ocampo's is the most important of those testimonies. "Mi deuda con Ortega" (same issue of *Sur*, 206–20) she gives a lively recapitulation of their friendship, their shared skepticism on politics, and their non-Hispanic literary tastes. (Victoria's interest in things Spanish diminished after she witnessed—as an adolescent—the goring of a horse in a bullfight.) Her essay includes excerpts from some of his letters. In "Algunas cartas de Ortega y Gasset," *Sur*, no. 296 (September–October, 1965), 1–18, she gives a fuller sampling of his correspondence from 1928 to 1941, including this excerpt from a letter dated October 28, 1940: "I'm alone most of the time, seeing nobody. It's the best period for productivity and lucidity I've ever had. It's only because my children are far away and *in Buenos Aires you can't find books* [my emphasis] that I'm not completely happy." (16)

Further light is cast on the Ocampo-Ortega friendship by Soledad Ortega (Ortega's daughter) in a May 15, 1979 tribute to Victoria Ocampo at UNESCO in Paris and reproduced in *Sur*, no. 346 (January–February, 1980): 15–22.

Two much earlier pieces are worthy of note: Francisco Romero, "Al margen de *La rebelión de las masas, Sur*, no. 2 (May, 1931): 192–205; and Manuel Gálvez, "Los argentinos según Ortega y Gasset" in *La Argentina y nuestros libros* (Santiago: Ediciones Ercilla, 1935), 107–9—the first for its intelligent interpretation of Ortega's view of twentieth-century value systems; the second for its criticism (albeit with overtones of social and racial intolerance) of Ortega's elitist excesses in judging Argentines.

Finally, in his introduction to *Hombres y engranajes* (1951), Ernesto Sábato refers as follows to Ortega's image of the mass-man: "Modern capitalism and positive science are two aspects of the same reality dispossessed of concrete attributes, of an abstract fantasizing that no longer belongs to the concrete individual man, but to the mass-man, that strange being truly enmeshed in a gigantic, anonymous machine." *Obra completa: Ensayos*, Ricardo Ibarlucía, ed. (Buenos Aires: Seix-Barral, 1997), 106. In the same work Sábato devotes a short essay to "Ortega y la deshumanización del arte," in which he proposes a theoretic reversal: "Proof of the dehumanization of art, for Ortega y Gasset, is found in the artist's divorce from the public. . . . I don't know why the Spanish philosopher didn't see that just the opposite could be true: that the public was the dehumanized party." (152)

28. *Nosotros*, 10, no. 87 (July, 1916): 110.

Chapter 6. Circling the Aleph

1. Julio Cortázar, "Del cuento breve y sus alrededores," in *Ultimo round*, 1, 8th ed. (Mexico City: Siglo XXI, 1983), 59–82.

2. "The Killers," in *The Short Stories of Ernest Hemingway* (New York: Charles Scribner's Sons, 1953), 284.

3. Eudora Welty, "Is Phoenix Jackson's Grandson Really Dead?" in the *Eye of the Story* (New York: Vintage Books, 1979), 160 and 161.

4. Rafael Arévalo Martínez, "El hombre que parecía un caballo" is reproduced in *An Anthology of Spanish American Literature*, 2nd ed., John E, Englekirk, Irving A. Leonard, John T. Reid, and John A. Crow, eds. (New York: Appeton-Century-Crofts, 1968), pp. 548–54.

5. Teresa Arévalo, *Rafael Arévalo Martínez, de 1884 hasta 1936* (Guatemala City: Tipografía Nacional, March, 1971), 270.

6. Jorge Luis Borges, "El aleph" in *Narraciones*, Marcos Ricardo Barnatán, ed. (Madrid: Ediciones Cátedra, 1990), 181.

7. Barnatán, the editor of *Narraciones*, reminds us in note 6 (ibid., 191) that the real Borges had used *Los naipes del tahur* as title for a collection of stories—never published—that he'd written as an adolescent.

8. Frieda Koeninger, "*El aleph*: sátira y parodia," in *Textos*, Columbia, SC, 4, no. 2 (1996): 37–41. Koeninger recalls that Borges' now famous stories gathered in *El jardín de los senderos que se bifurcan* got "only one vote" in the 1942 competition for the National Prize (37).

9. Harold Bloom, "Borges, Neruda, and Pessoa: Hispanic-Portuguese Whitman," in *The Western Canon* (New York: First Riverhead Edition, 1995), 448.

10. Luisa Valenzuela, "Los censores," reproduced in Raquel Chang-Rodríguez and Malva E. Filer, eds. *Voces de Hispanoamérica* (Boston: Heinle & Heinle Publishers, 1987), 514–15.

11. Luisa Valenzuela, *Cambio de armas* (Hanover, N.H.: Ediciones del Norte, 1982), 123–24.

12. Julio Ortega, "Prólogo" in *El muro y la intemperie* (Hanover, N.H.: Ediciones del Norte, 1989), x.

13. As he flees, the pursued man refers to the weight of his conscience and his physical vulnerability. "Any eye that finds me can see that weight; it'll look like a strange swelling. That's what I feel." More obvious as a clue, of course, would be the missing toe: "others noticed it but I didn't, until later." Juan Rulfo, *El llano en llamas*, 2nd ed. (Mexico City: Fondo de Cultura Económica, 1955), 45.

14. Horacio Quiroga, "El hombre muerto," in *Horacio Quiroga: sus mejores cuentos*, John A. Crow, ed. (Mexico City: Editorial Cvltvra, 1943), 228–33.

15. Julio Cortázar, "las babas del Diablo," in *Las armas secretas*, 5th ed., Susana Jakfalvi, ed. (Madrid: Cátedra, 1984), 129.

16. Gabriel Garcia Marquez, "Un hombre muy viejo con unas alas enormes," in *Literatura hispanoamericana*, vol. 2, Enrique Anderson Imbert and Eugenio Florit, eds. (New York: Holt, Rinehart and Winston, 1970), 414–16. The story first appeared in the journal *Casa de las Américas*, Havana, 8 (May–June, 1968).

Chapter 7. As the Fly Spies

1. *Encyclopedia of the Essay*, Tracy Chevalier, ed. (London: Fitzroy Dearborn Publishers, 1997).

2. Graham Good, Preface to *The Observing Self: Rediscovering the Essay* (London: Routledge, 1988), vii.

3. Robert Atwan, "Essayism," *The Iowa Review*, vol. 25, no. 2 (1995): 7.

4. Jacques Derrida, in "*Il n'y a pas de hors-texte*," *De la grammatologie* (Paris: Les Éditions de Minuit, 1967), 227. The italics were Derrida's own.

5. Umberto Eco, "Preface to the American Edition," in *Travels in Hyperreality*, William Weaver, Trans. (San Diego, Ca.: Harcourt Brace Jovanovich, 1986), xi.

6. José Luis Gómez-Martínez, "El ensayo y las formas de expresión afines," in *Teoría del ensayo* (Mexico City: UNAM, 1992), 105–25.

7. Juan Loveluck, "El ensayo hispanoamericano y su naturaleza," *Los Ensayistas,* 1 (1976): 7–13.

8. Enrique Anderson Imbert, *La originalidad de Rubén Darío* (Buenos Aires: Centro Editor de América Latina, 1967), 281.

9. Donald Kalish, "Semantics," in *The Encyclopedia of Philosophy,* ed. Paul Edwards (New York: Macmillan, 1972), 8: 348.

10. W. V. Quine, "Notes on a Theory of Reference," in *From a Logical Point of View* (Cambridge, Mass., 1967), 130–38.

11. Ernesto Sábato, *Abaddón el exterminador* in *Obra completa: Narrativa,* Ricardo Ibarlucía, ed. (Buenos Aires: Seix-Barral, 1997), 670.

12. Rosario Ferré, *Eccentric Neighborhoods* (New York: Penguin Putnam, Inc. 1999). Rosario Ferré has written most of her works to date in Spanish. This novel was originally done in English.

13. See James Willis Robb's introduction, "Siete presencias de Alfonso Reayes," to his edition *Prosa y poesía* (Madrid: EdicionesCátedra, 1975), 11–24.

14. Octavio Paz, "Los signos en rotación," epilogue to *El arco y la lira,* 2nd ed. (Mexico City: Fondo de Cultura Económica, 1967), 260.

15. Ortega's intended meaning of *ciencia,* in his celebrated dictum, includes philosophy. It was written in defense of his own method, in the prologue to *Meditaciones del Quijote* (1914). In it he insisted on the existence of proof—at least in the writer's mind. Accordingly, the writer's poetic license would consist of an ellipsis: essays "are not philosophy, which is science. They're simply essays. And the essay is science, less its explicit proof. The writer must demonstrate intellectual honor by not writing anything subject to proof unless he already has the proof. But he is allowed to eliminate from his work all appearances of the incontestable (*lo apodíctico*), merely indicating the proofs in such a way that whoever needs them can find them and that they don't prevent an expansion of the intimacy in which those thoughts were realized." *Meditaciones del Quijote* (Madrid: Revista de Occidente, 1960), 12.

Right here we see Ortega's fallacy. He has said in effect that creative writing is covert philosophy, that the writer—for all his "intellectual honor"—subjects the reader to a cover-up by removing from his text all "appearances of the incontestable," and that if the reader takes the trouble to dig through the outer layers of literature he will find Ortega's sleeping beauty underneath: philosophy. In the depth of his creative soul Ortega surely felt that there was more than that.

16. Lionel Trilling, *The Liberal Imagination* (New York: Doubleday, 1953), 273.

17. Alfonso Reyes, *La experiencia literaria* (Buenos Aires: Losada, 1969), 73–74.

Chapter 8. Spain's Edgy Generation

1. As a philosopher, Ortega seems to be shifting the balance found in the *Oxford English Dictionary*'s definition of *Intellectualism* ("The doctrine that knowledge is wholly or mainly derived from the action of the intellect, i.e., from pure reason") to his own synthesis of rationality and intuitiveness.

2. On Baroja's uncompromising pessimism see Peter Earle, "Baroja y su ética de la imposibilidad" in *Cuadernos Hispanoamericanos,* nos. 265–67 (July–September, 1972).

3. The stylistic and idealistic gap between the nineteenth-century realists and

the Generation of 1898 is punctuated by Dorio de Gadex's denigrating allusion in scene 4 of Valle Inclán's *Luces de Bohemia* to Pérez Galdós as "Don Benito the Chickpea Dealer."

4. As for the Generation of 1898, Unamuno (1864), Valle-Inclán (1866), Baroja (1872), Azorín (1874), Machado (1875), and Maeztu (1875), were all born within eleven years; so Baroja's proposed label of a "Generation of 1870" was quite accurate as far as proximity of birth is concerned.

Chapter 9: In and Out of Time

1. I say "composite" in the sense that the unnamed, superannuated patriarch of the novel embodied traits of several legendary Hispanic dictators, including José Gaspar Rodríguez (alias "Dr. Francia" and "El Supremo") of Paraguay, Juan Vicente Gómez of Venezuela, Manuel Estrada Cabrera of Guatemala, Rafael Trujillo of the Dominican Republic, and General Francisco Franco of Spain who, physically as well as symbolically, succumbed to his prolonged illness in 1975, the year that *El otoño del Patriarca* was published.

2. "Fiction shows us the past as well as the present moment in mortal light; it is an art served by the indelibility of our memory." "Some Notes on Time in Fiction," 1973, reproduced in Eudora Welty, *The Eye of the Story* (NY: Vintage Books, 1979), 168.

3. In *Vivir para contarla* (NY: Alfred A. Knopf, 2002), 22, the first volume of his autobiography, García Márquez reminds us that Macondo was a real place. When he was twenty-two he saw the word written—while passing by on the train—on the gateway entrance to a deserted banana plantation near Aracataca, his native town.

4. World War II had not yet begun, but in March 1939 Germany occupied Czechoslovakia militarily, declaring it, in Adolph Hitler's euphemism, a "protectorate."

5. Quotations from *The Idiot* are from Alan Myers's translation (New York: Oxford University Press, 1992).

6. Cases of a perpetual present or mysterious time lapses in "real life" are not hard to find. For example, astronauts regularly attest to a loss of sense of time caused by their altered "bio-rhythms" in gravity-free space. Day and night merge, they say, and calendars and clocks are irrelevant when one is stationed or moving in orbit for an extended period.

The emotions can also be decisive in the suspension of time. Anne Morrow Lindbergh (1906–2001), a talented testimonial writer as well as the wife and copilot of a celebrity—refers to the kidnapping and death of their first child in 1932 in this way: "Everything since then has been unreal. It has all vanished in smoke. Only that *eternal moment* [my emphasis] remains. I feel strangely a sense of peace—not peace, but an end to restlessness, a finality, as though I were sleeping in a grave." (Quoted by Eric Pace in "Anne Morrow Lindbergh is Dead at 94," *New York Times*, February 8, 2001, A29).

7. This work in progress (*Transformaciones*), we should note, is only the tip of the *primo*'s bibliographical iceberg. Another of his projects is a treatise on *libreas* (servant uniforms)—703 of them, no less—written to cover all levels of service protocol and profusely illustrated, and two more tomes equally deserving of oblivion. Is Cervantes, who minutely parodies the chivalric style and motifs in the Montesinos

chapters and many others, also taking a swing at the practitioners of intricate academic writing in his era (who are curiously similar to those of later eras)?

8. Quotations (my translation) are taken from Martín de Riquer's edition of Cervantes, *Don Quijote* (New York: Las Américas Publishing Company, 1958).

9. The time-and-space scramble that often perturbs Don Quijote is also a factor in Graham Greene's reincarnation of the old knight in *Monsignor Quixote* (1981). In that work Father Quixote is a priest from El Toboso faithfully followed throughout by Enrique Zancas, a Communist ex-mayor of the same town. The Monsignor's mental state evolves in the opposite direction of Don Quijote's, i.e., from calm rationality toward a lucid kind of madness. He lives his final hours in a delirium of feverish gestures and words, including irreverent remarks about some of his fellow clergymen, a convoluted rendering of the Mass in Latin, and the solemn declaration that "a fart can be musical."

10. In Alan Trueblood, *INTI*, no. 45 (Spring 1997): 85–94

11. Quoted by William Leatherbarrow in his introduction to *The Idiot* (New York: Oxford University Press, 1992).

12. Translations of this and subsequent brief passages from Jorge Luis Borges, *Ficciones* (Buenos Aires: Emecé, 1963) are my own.

13. In a note appearing in "The New Geography of Classic Spanish Literature," *The Chronicle of Higher Education* (Feb. 2, 2001), Scott Heller refers to Diana de Armas Wilson's book, *Cervantes, the Novel, and the New World*, and comments that "Ms. Wilson is among the scholars trying to circumvent an us-versus-them scenario by calling for a 'transatlantic literary study, reading Spanish texts in relation to the New World.'" I'm grateful to Professor Carlos J. Alonso for referring me to Heller's note and Armas Wilson's book.

CHAPTER 10. MARTÍ, VASCONCELOS, MISTRAL

1. The letter is reproduced in *Obras completas* (Havana: Editorial Nacional de Cuba, 1963–73), 10:225–32. Subsequent quotations from this edition are in my translation.

2. Ivan Schulman and Manuel Pedro González, *Martí, Darío y el modernismo* (Madrid: Editorial Gredos, 1969), 32.

3. This passage (my translation) is from an article signed June 26, 1886 in New York and later published in *El Partido Liberal* of Mexico City. The article is reproduced in *Nuevas cartas de Nueva York*, (Ernesto Mejía Sánchez), ed. (Mexico City: Siglo XXI, 1980), 38–43. Martí published 146 articles in *El partido Liberal* between 1886 and 1892. These were in addition to numerous others in *La Nación* of Buenos Aires (1881–92), *La República* (Honduras), *La Opinión Pública* (Montevideo) and—in English—*The Hour* and *The Sun* (New York)

4. Heníquez Ureña, *Las corrientes literarias en la América Hispánica* (Mexico City: Fondo de Cultura Económica, 1949), 168.

5. *The Oxford History of the American People* (New York: Oxford University Press, 1965), 773.

6. See: Gabriela Mistral, *Bendita mi lengua sea*, vol. 1 (Jaime Quezada, ed. (Santiago, Chile: Editorial Sudamericana, 1999), 93.

7. Significantly Vasconcelos, portrayed early in 1928 by a reporter of *The New York Times* as "the only Mexican civilian who could be elected by popular vote,"

NOTES 177

represents with Vicente Fox the beginning and end of the PRI (Partido Revolucionario Institucional) dynasty. For Fox, candidate of the Partido de Acción Nacional, the election process in July 2000 was carefully observed and recorded. By contrast, after several of Vasconcelos's supporters were killed during the 1929 campaign, the results were systematically falsified. Pascal Ortiz Rubio, a simple "strongman's shadow" of Calles, was one more unqualified military figure of the caste that Vasconcelos would denounce the rest of his life.

8. We should remember that Vasconcelos considered Cortés—not Cuauhtémoc or Moctezuma—as the true founder of the Mexican nation.

9. The proconsolute referred to in the title was that of Dwight W. Morrow (1873–1931), the U.S. Ambassador to Mexico from 1927 to 1929. According to *The Columbia Encyclopedia* Morrow's service "was notable because it marked a new spirit in U.S. relations with Latin America." *The Columbia Encyclopedia*, 3rd ed. (New York: Columbia University Press, 1963), p. 1424. But in *El proconsulado* Vasconcelos expresses a very different evaluation, alleging that the ambassador blatantly conspired with Vasconcelos's corrupt opposition to defeat him in the 1929 election.

10. For a succinct and sensitive biography of Rivas Mercado, including her anguished last days, see *Antonieta* by Fabienne Bradu (Mexico City: Fondo de Cultura Económica, 1991).

11. What has been preserved of her work is published in *Obras completas de María Antonieta Rivas Mercado*, Luis Mario Schneider, ed. (Mexico City: Ediciones Oasis, 1987).

12. See "Malgré tout," one of the chapters on Spain near the end of Vascondelos, *El proconsulado*.

13. Gabriela Mistral, "El voto femenino," in *Escritos políticos*, selection, prologue and notes by Jaime Quezada (Santiago, Chile: Fondo de Cultura Económica, 1994), 265.

14. See Doris Meyer, *Victoria Ocampo. Against the Wind and the Tide* (New York: George Braziller, 1979), 161.

15. Donald Hall, *The Poet as Critic* (Evanston, Ill.: Northwestern University Press, 1967), 85.

16. See Saul Yurkievich, *Fundadores de la nueva poesía latinoamericana* (Barcelona: Barral Editores, 1978).

17. Humberto Díaz-Casanueva, "Evocación de Gabriela Mistral," in *Gabriela Mistral*, ed. Mirella Servodidio and Marcelo Coddou (Universidad Veracruzana, 1980), 12.

Index